SEW A
Winter Woodland
CHRISTMAS

Mix & Match 20 Paper-Pieced Blocks
9 Projects

Mary Hertel

C&T PUBLISHING
Another Maker Inspired!

Text copyright © 2024 by Mary Ann Hertel

Photography and artwork copyright © 2024 by C&T Publishing, Inc.

Publisher: Amy Barrett-Daffin

Creative Director: Gailen Runge

Senior Editor: Roxane Cerda

Technical Editor: Helen Frost

Cover/Book Designer: April Mostek

Production Coordinator: Tim Manibusan

Illustrator: Aliza Shalit and Valyrie Gillum

Photography Coordinator: Rachel Ackley

Front cover photography by Paula Shoultz

Subjects and styled photography by Paula Shoultz; instructional photography by
C&T Publishing, Inc., unless otherwise noted

Published by C&T Publishing, Inc., P.O. Box 1456, Lafayette, CA 94549

Library of Congress Cataloging-in-Publication Data

Names: Hertel, Mary, 1955- author.

Title: Sew a winter woodland christmas : mix & match 20 paper-pieced blocks, 9 projects / Mary
Hertel.

Description: Lafayette, CA : C&T Publishing, [2024] | Summary: "Learn how to make twenty
adorable creatures blocks with a wintery twist and nine projects that would make excellent
holiday gifts. This book offers paper piecing step-by-step instructions for beginners and loads
of enjoyable

patterns for intermediate quilters"-- Provided by publisher.

Identifiers: LCCN 2023050919 | ISBN 9781644034842 (trade paperback) | ISBN
9781644034859 (ebook)

Subjects: LCSH: Patchwork--Patterns. | Quilting--Patterns. | Patchwork quilts. | Sewing.

Classification: LCC TT835 .H44689 2023 | DDC 746.46--dc23/eng/20231205

LC record available at https://lccn.loc.gov/2023050919

Printed in the USA

10 9 8 7 6 5 4 3 2

Dedication

I dedicate this book to my best friend, partner, and sounding board, Tom. He always keeps me on the right track.

Acknowledgments

Thank you to my family and friends. I love you all.

Contents

Introduction—6

Paper-Piecing Basics—7

Tools • Things to Know • Preparing the Patterns • Paper Piecing Segment A • Joining Segments • Joining Blocks

PROJECTS 12

Introduction

Get ready for some frosty fun!
There's something special about a
winter quilt. Let's embrace winter
with my newest block patterns.
Paper piece winter-themed projects
with these adorable blocks. All 20
blocks feature charming animals
with snow caps, scarves, and other
wintery items. Capture the spirit of
the season with these nine gorgeous
winter projects to warm your heart
and hearth. The projects include a
lap quilt, table runner, tree skirt,
zippered pouch, pillow, gift bag,
apron, and—my favorites—kitten
and puppy Christmas stockings.

This book includes step-by-step
instructions for paper piecing, nine
cozy and cute projects, and 20
adorable block patterns. Some of the
blocks are 8″ × 8″ squares, and some
are a combination of 2 square blocks
sewn together, which result in a
rectangular block that is 8″ × 15½″.

As in my previous books, the block
patterns are interchangeable in all
the projects. Plus, these blocks will
also fit into the projects from my
previous seven books. That means
that you can conceivably create
hundreds of projects by using my
books. You can be super-creative!

Photo by Gail Cameron

Paper-Piecing Basics

Tools

- Paper (Carol Doak's Foundation Paper by C&T Publishing recommended)

- Sharp scissors

- Rotary cutter and mat

- Ruler with an easy-to-read ¼″ line (such as Add-A-Quarter ruler by CM Designs)

- Multipurpose tool (such as Alex Anderson's 4-in-1 Essential Sewing Tool by C&T Publishing) or seam ripper

- Flat-head straight pins

- Lamp or light source (window)

- Sewing machine

- Iron and ironing board

Things to Know

STITCH LENGTH

Set the stitch length at 1.5, which is about 20 stitches per inch. The stitch perforations must be close together to allow the paper to rip easily, but not so close that ripping out a seam is an impossible task.

PREPARE A CONVENIENT WORK STATION

Have the iron, ironing board, and cutting mat close to the sewing machine. A light source should be handy for positioning scrap pieces on the back of the pattern. A window works well during the day, and a lamp suffices at night.

THE BUTTERFLY EFFECT

After you sew a seamline, flip the fabric behind the numbered piece on the pattern that you are currently attaching. This motion creates a butterfly effect, meaning that the fabric scrap needs to be lined up to the seam in such a way that it will cover the space you are sewing after it is flipped into place. If you are concerned that the size of your scrap is insufficient, pin along the seamline and try flipping the scrap into place before sewing the seam. That way, if the scrap does not cover the area sufficiently, you can adjust it or find a larger scrap.

FOLLOW ALONG

If you are new to paper piecing, follow along for practice by using the Red Truck with Snowman block, Part 1 (page 75), as you read the following instructions.

Preparing the Patterns

1 Make the recommended number of color copies of the original block. (You need 3 copies for the Red Truck with Snowman, Part 1, block.)

2 Cut the block into the segments denoted by the capital letters, *adding ¼" seam allowances along the red lines and the outside edges of the block.* For the example, use one copy for Segments A and C and one copy each for Segments B and D.

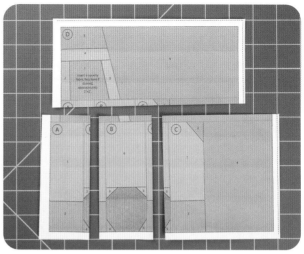

Segments A, B, C, and D with ¼" seam allowances around outside edges

Paper Piecing Segment A

Always stitch pieces in numerical order. Don't forget to set your stitch length to 1.5, or about 20 stitches per inch.

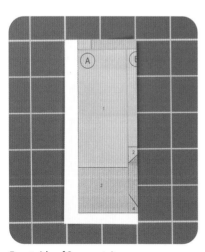

Front side of Segment A

1 Pin the *wrong* side of the Piece 1 fabric onto the *unprinted* side of the paper pattern. The right side of the fabric faces you (away from the paper).

2 Bend the paper pattern and fabric along the seamline between Pieces 1 and 2. Use a heavy piece of tagboard, such as a bookmark or postcard, to make the fold. Doing so will help you line up the fabric for Piece 2.

3 Trim the fabric behind Piece 1 to ¼″ with the Add-A-Quarter ruler.

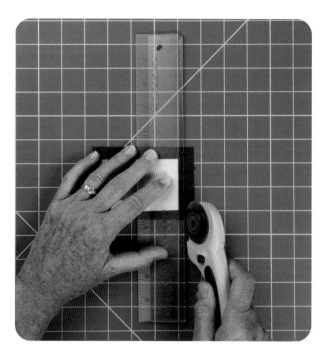

4 Keeping the pattern bent back along the seamline, align the Piece 2 fabric with the Fabric from Piece 1. The fabric for Piece 2 will be flipped into place after sewing. Pin in place, right sides together.

Right Sides Together   *As you are piecing, the right sides of the fabric should always be together.*

5 Flip the pattern flat and sew ¼″ beyond the seamline at the beginning and the end of this seam (as shown by the green line). No backtacking is needed, as the ends of the seams are stitched over by other seams. Notice that the fabric for Piece 2 is much larger than needed; it will be trimmed later.

Double-Check to Avoid Seam Ripping

I like to use large scraps (but no larger than 9″ × 11″) and then trim the piece after sewing it in place. As you place the fabric under your presser foot to sew, the seam allowance and the shape you are filling should be to your right. The shape you previously completed should be to your left. Before sewing, do a mental check. Ask yourself these two questions: "Is the piece I am working on to my right?" and "Is the majority of my fabric to my left?" If the answer is yes to both, then sew. This simple check will eliminate much seam ripping.

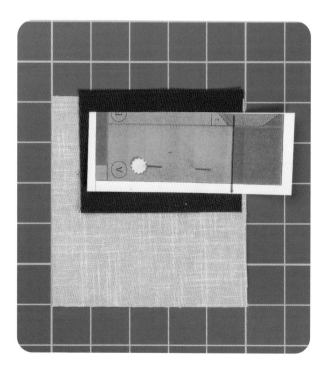

6 Flip the fabric into position behind Piece 2 and press. Pin in place to keep it flat.

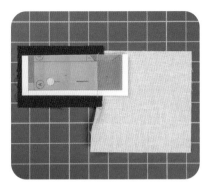

7 Trim the fabric a generous ½″ beyond the first edge of Piece 2 (see dotted lines). *Do not cut the pattern.*

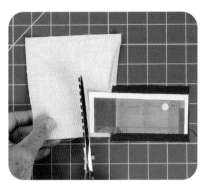

8 Trim the fabric a generous ½″ beyond the second edge of Piece 2.

9 Segment A is finished, but if a segment has more than two pieces, continue to add the remaining pieces in the same manner that you added Piece 2.

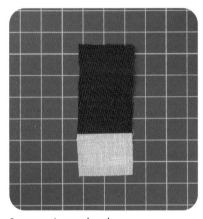

Segment A completed

10 Trim the seam allowance of Segment A to an *exact* ¼″ seam by using a rotary cutter, a mat, and a ruler with a ¼″ line. The segment is now ready to be sewn to the other segments. Follow the same process to make Segments B, C, and D.

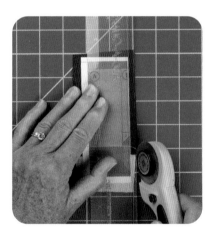

Joining Segments

Note: Make sure that each segment is trimmed so that it has an exact ¼″ seam allowance along the red segment seamline only. Do not trim the outer edge seam allowances at this time.

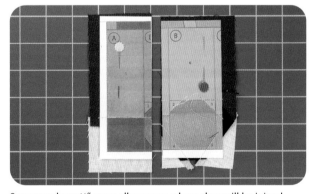

Segments have ¼″ seam allowances where they will be joined.

1 With right sides together, pin together the edges of Segments A and B, matching the red sewing lines. Push a straight pin through the end of each red line to help align them as closely as possible. Sew on the red line and ¼″ past the red line on both ends.

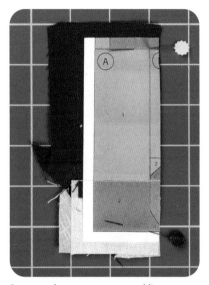

Sew together segments on red line.

2 Remove the paper from the seam allowance to eliminate the possibility of the paper getting trapped under the seams.

3 Press the seam to the side. Let the seam "show" you in which direction it wants to be pressed.

Continue joining segments until Red Truck with Snowman, Part 1, is complete. Repeat the process of paper piecing, beginning with Preparing the Patterns (page 8), for Red Truck with Snowman, Part 2 (page 76).

Joining Blocks

Blue lines join completed blocks. Unlike red segment seams, blue line seams are backtacked at the beginning and end.

1 Trim only the edges on Parts 1 and 2 that have a *blue* line. Trim these edges ¼″ away from the blue line.

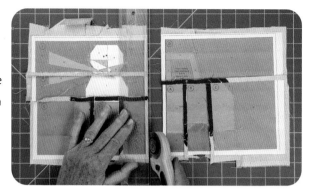

2 Pin the Parts 1 and 2 blocks right sides together, matching the blue lines.

3 Sew on the blue line and backtack at the beginning and end of the seam. Rip the paper from the seam area. Press the block open.

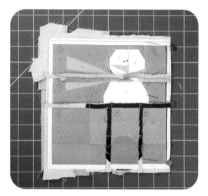

> **Finish Before Trimming**
>
> *Make sure to never trim the excess fabric from the outer edges of the block until the block is finished and joined to its partner block. After that, it is safe to square up the block with a cutting mat, ruler, and rotary cutter. A rectangular block should measure 8″ × 15½″, unfinished.*

4 Complete any embroidery *while* the paper is still attached. The paper acts as a stabilizer and will keep the block from stretching. *After* the block has been attached to the project, the paper may be removed.

Lap Quilt

FINISHED SIZE: 46½″ × 66″

Materials

Fabric A: 1 yard for sashing

Fabric B: 1¼ yards for border

Fabric C: ⅝ yard for binding

Fabric D: 3 yards for backing

Fabrics E and F: 1 yard each of 2 background fabrics for paper-pieced blocks

Assorted scraps: For paper piecing 18 blocks *(See your selected block's materials list.)*

Batting: 1½ yards 90″ wide

Cutting

Yardages are based on 42″ usable width of fabric (WOF). Fold fabric selvage to selvage.

Fabric A

• Cut 14 strips 2″ × WOF.

• Subcut 12 rectangles 2″ × 8″.

• Subcut 7 strips 2″ × 33½″.

• Set aside 4 strips for the side sashing.

Fabric B

• Cut 6 strips 5½″ × WOF.

Fabric C

• Cut 7 strips 2½″ × WOF.

Fabric D

• Cut 3 yards of fabric in half, each piece 1½ yards long.

Sewing

Use ¼″ seams throughout unless otherwise directed.

PAPER-PIECED BLOCKS

Refer to Paper-Piecing Basics (page 7) as needed.

1 Paper piece 12 square blocks and 6 rectangular blocks of your choosing (from Pattern Blocks, pages 52–78), using Fabrics E and F as the background fabrics and the assorted scraps for the rest of the block. *(See your selected block's materials list.)*

2 Add any necessary embroidery.

3 Trim each square block to 8″ × 8″. Trim each rectangular block to 8″ × 15½″.

SEW THE SASHING TO THE BLOCKS

Each of the 6 rows consists of 2 square blocks, 1 rectangular block, and 2 Fabric A 2″ × 8″ sashing strips.

1 Rows 1 and 6: Sew Fabric A 2″ × 8″ sashing strips to the side of a square block and a rectangular block. Sew the 3 blocks together. Press the seams toward the sashing.

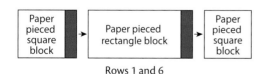

Rows 1 and 6

2 Rows 2 and 4: Sew Fabric A 2″ × 8″ sashing strips to the side of a rectangular block and a square block. Sew the 3 blocks together. Press the seams toward the sashing.

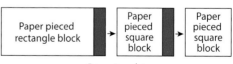

Rows 2 and 4

3 Rows 3 and 5: Sew Fabric A 2″ × 8″ sashing strips to the side of 2 square blocks. Sew the 3 blocks together. Press the seams toward the sashing.

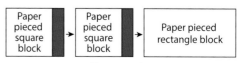

Rows 3 and 5

4 Sew a Fabric A 2″ × 33½″ sashing strip to the top and bottom of Row 1 and to just the bottom of Row 6. Press the seams toward the sashing.

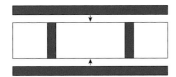

Sew sashing to top and bottom of Row 1.

5 Sew a Fabric A 2″ × 33½″ sashing strip to the bottom of Rows 2 and 4. Repeat for Rows 3 and 5. Press the seams toward the sashing. Sew rows 1-5 together. Press the seams towards the sashing.

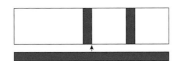

Sew strips to bottom of Rows 2 and 4.

Sew strips to bottom of Rows 3 and 5.

6 Sew the 4 remaining Fabric A 2″ × WOF sashing strips together in pairs to make 2 extra-long strips. Sew each extra-long strip to the side edges of the quilt. Press the seams toward the sashing.

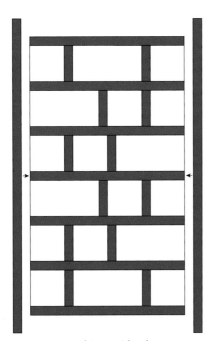

Sew sashing to side edges.

7 Trim the excess fabric from both ends of the sashing strips.

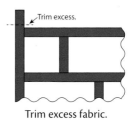

Trim excess fabric.

ATTACH THE BORDER

1 Sew a Fabric B 5½″ × WOF strip to the top and bottom edges of the quilt. Trim the excess fabric.

2 Sew the 4 remaining Fabric B 5½″ × WOF sashing strips together in pairs to make 2 longer strips. Sew each longer strip to the side edges of the quilt. Trim the excess fabric.

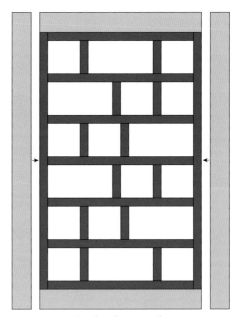

Sew borders to quilt.

QUILTING

1 Remove the paper from the back of the blocks.

2 Sew together the 2 Fabric D pieces, selvage to selvage, with ¾" seams. Trim off the selvages in the seam allowance. Press open.

3 Layer the Fabric D prepared backing (right side facing down), batting, and quilt top (right side facing up).

4 Pin all 3 layers together and quilt as desired.

BINDING

1 Pin together 2 Fabric C 2½" × WOF binding strips, overlapping on a right angle and with the right sides together. Mark a diagonal line from Corner A to Corner B. Sew on the diagonal line to connect the strips.

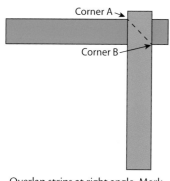

Overlap strips at right angle. Mark diagonal line.

2 Trim the seam to ¼" and press to one side. Continue, adding the rest of the strips to make one continuous strip.

3 Press the strip in half lengthwise, with the wrong sides together.

4 Beginning at the center of one side, align the raw edges of the binding strip with the raw edges of the quilt. Fold the beginning of the strip at a 90-degree angle (right angle), with the tail facing away from the quilt.

5 Stitch ¼" from the raw edges. Stop stitching ¼" from the first corner and backtack.

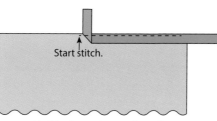

Pin binding strip to quilt and start stitching here.

6 Fold the binding strip straight up. The raw edge of the binding strip should align with the raw edge of the second side of the quilt.

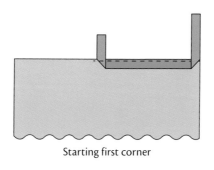

Starting first corner

7 Fold the binding strip straight down to overlap the second edge of the quilt. Start stitching at the top corner and continue until ¼" from the next corner, then backtack.

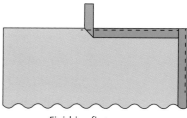

Finishing first corner

8 Continue in this manner around the remaining sides of the quilt, backtacking and turning at each corner.

9 Trim the end of the binding strip so it overlaps the angled beginning section by 2". Trim the remaining tail ends.

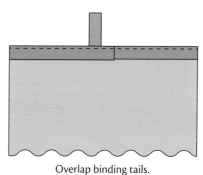

Overlap binding tails.

10 Press the binding around to the back of the quilt and hand stitch in place, easing in the fullness where the tails overlap.

Foxy Tree Skirt

FINISHED SIZE: 30½" × 30½"

Materials

Fabric A: 1 yard for sashing and binding

Fabric B: 1 yard for rectangles, triangles, and center square

Fabric C: ½ yard for background fabric for paper-pieced blocks

Fabric D: 1¼ yards for backing

Assorted scraps: For paper piecing (*See your selected block's materials list.*)

Batting: 40″ × 40″ square

Cutting

Yardages are based on 42″ usable width of fabric (WOF). Fold fabric selvage to selvage.

Fabric A

• Cut 4 strips 1½″ × WOF.

• Subcut 8 strips 1½″ × 8″ and 8 strips 1½″ × 10″ for sashing.

• Cut 7 strips 2½″ × WOF for ties and binding.

• Subcut 2 of the strips in half to make 4 pieces 2″ × 20″ for ties.

Fabric B

• Cut 1 strip 3″ × WOF.

• Subcut into 4 rectangles 3″ × 10″.

• Cut 1 square 10″ × 10″.

• Cut 1 square 18¼″ × 18¼″. Subcut diagonally in both directions to create 4 triangles.

Sewing

Use ¼″ seams throughout unless otherwise directed.

PAPER-PIECED BLOCKS

Refer to Paper-Piecing Basics (page 7) as needed.

1 Paper piece 4 selected square blocks (from Pattern Blocks, pages 52–78), using Fabric C for the background and the assorted scraps for the rest of each block. (*See your selected block's materials list.*)

2 Add any necessary embroidery.

3 Trim the blocks to 8″ × 8″.

SEW SASHING TO THE BLOCKS

1 Sew the Fabric A 1½″ × 8″ sashing strips to the top and bottom of each paper-pieced block. Press the seams toward the sashing.

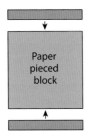

Sew strips to top and bottom of blocks.

2 Sew the Fabric A 1½″ × 10″ sashing strips to the sides of each paper-pieced block. Press the seams toward the sashing.

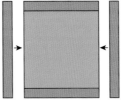

Sew strips to sides of blocks.

CONSTRUCT EACH ROW

1 Sew a Fabric B 3″ × 10″ rectangle to the bottom of each block.

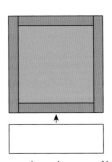

Sew rectangles to bottom of blocks.

2 Sew Fabric B triangles to the side edges of 2 of the blocks. The right angle of each triangle should align with the top corners of the block. Press the seams open.

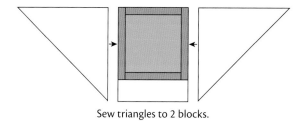

Sew triangles to 2 blocks.

3 Sew the top edge of the 2 remaining blocks to the sides of the Fabric B 10″ square. Press the seams open.

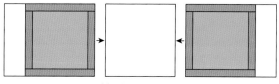

Sew 2 blocks to center square.

ASSEMBLE THE ROWS

1 Sew the 3 rows together as shown. Press the seams open.

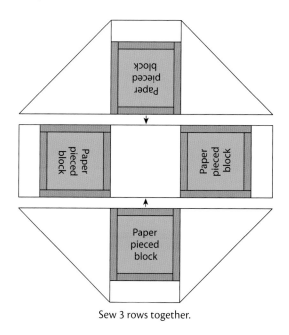

Sew 3 rows together.

QUILTING

1 Remove the paper from the back of the blocks.

2 Trace the circle template (page 22) in the center of the tree skirt. On the tree skirt, draw a straight line from the edge of the circle, between the corners of 2 blocks, and to the center of the edge triangle.

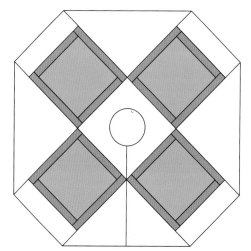

Mark circle and straight line on tree skirt.

3 Layer the Fabric D backing (right side facing down), batting, and tree skirt (right side facing up).

4 Secure the layers with pins. Quilt as desired through all the layers.

5 Cut on the straight line, but don't cut out the circle. It is easier to bind the circle before cutting.

SEW THE TIES

1 Fold each Fabric A 2½″ × 20″ strip in half lengthwise. Sew along the long edge. Turn each strip right side out, using a safety pin or bodkin. Press flat, with the seam going down the center of each tie.

Sew long edge of ties.

2 Hem one end of each tie by folding it under ¼″ twice. Press and stitch the end.

Sew hem on one end of ties.

3 Pin 2 ties to each straight edge, right sides together, with the raw edge of the ties aligning with the seam allowance. Pin the first ties 2½″ from the circle. Pin the second ties 4½″ from the first ties. Baste the ties in place along the seamline. Pin the length of the tie out of the way for sewing the binding in place.

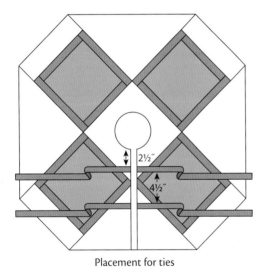

Placement for ties

BINDING

1 Using the Fabric A 2½″ × WOF strips, pin 2 strips together, overlapping at a right angle, right sides together. Mark a diagonal line from Corner A to Corner B.

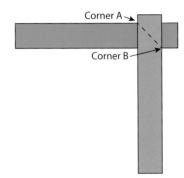

Overlap strips at right angle. Mark diagonal line.

2 Sew on the diagonal line. Trim seams to ¼″. Press seams to one side. Continue adding the rest of the strips to make 1 continuous strip.

3 Press the strips in half lengthwise with the wrong sides together.

4 Fold the beginning of the binding strip on a 90-degree angle (right angle), with the tail facing away from the tree skirt.

5 Stitch ¼″ from the raw edges. Stop stitching ¼″ from the first corner and backtack.

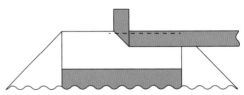

Pin binding strip to tree skirt and start stitching here.

6 Fold the binding strip up at an angle. The raw edge of the binding strip should align with the raw edge of the adjacent edge of the tree skirt.

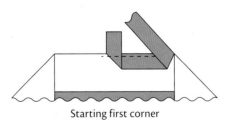

Starting first corner

7 Fold the binding strip straight down to overlap the second edge of the tree skirt. Start stitching at the top edge and continue until ¼″ from the next corner, then backtack.

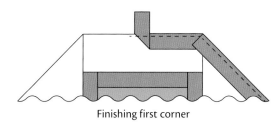

Finishing first corner

8 Continue in this manner around the remaining edges of the tree skirt, backtacking and turning at each corner and continuing along the cut edges and around the marked center circle.

9 Trim the end of the binding strip so it overlaps the angled beginning section by 1″. Trim the remaining tail ends.

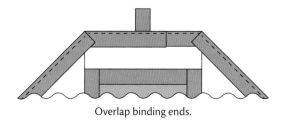

Overlap binding ends.

10 Cut out the center circle and trim the excess backing and batting on the edges.

11 Press the binding around to the back of the tree skirt and hand stitch in place, easing in the fullness where the tails overlap.

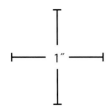

1″

Use ruler to measure
these inch marks to verify that
printout is correctly sized.

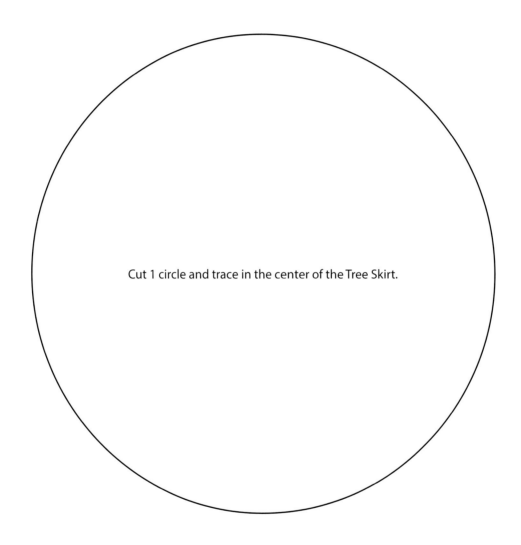

Cut 1 circle and trace in the center of the Tree Skirt.

Ruffled Apron

FINISHED APRON SIZE: 25" × 32"

Materials

Fabric A: 1 yard for main fabric

Fabric B: 1½ yards for lining, pocket, and ruffle

Fusible batting: 8″ × 18″

Assorted scraps: For paper piecing (*See your selected block's materials list.*)

Ribbon: 4 yards 1″ wide grosgrain

Cutting

Yardages are based on 42″ usable width of fabric (WOF). Fold fabric selvage to selvage.

Fabric A

• Cut 1 rectangle 26″ × 29″.

Fabric B

• Cut 1 rectangle 26″ × 29″ for lining.

• Cut 2 rectangles 5½″ × 8″ for pocket; cut 1 rectangle 18″ × 8″ for pocket lining.

• Cut 1 strip 9″ × WOF for ruffle.

Sewing

Use ¼″ seams throughout unless otherwise directed.

PAPER-PIECED BLOCK

Refer to Paper-Piecing Basics (page 7) as needed.

1 Paper piece 1 square block of your choosing (from Pattern Blocks, pages 52–78), using the assorted scraps. (*See your selected block's materials list.*)

2 Add any necessary embroidery.

3 Trim the block to 8″ × 8″.

CONSTRUCT THE FRONT OF THE POCKET

1 Sew the Fabric B 5½″ × 8″ rectangles to the sides of the paper-pieced block, right sides together. Press the seam toward Fabric B.

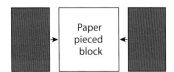

Add pieces to sides of block.

2 Remove the paper from the back of the paper-pieced block.

3 Steam press the fusible batting to the back of the paper-pieced unit.

4 With right sides together, sew the Fabric B 18″ × 8″ lining piece to the paper-pieced unit, leaving a 6″ opening along the bottom edge. Turn the unit right side out, gently poking out the corners. Hand sew to close the opening.

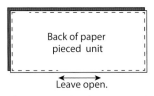

Sew lining to pocket, leaving opening.

5 Quilt the pocket as desired.

CONSTRUCT THE FRONT OF THE APRON

1 Pin the Fabric A 26″ × 29″ piece to the Fabric B lining piece, right sides together.

2 Place the pinned fabric on a cutting mat and measure 6″ over and 10″ down from the top corners. Draw a diagonal line to connect the two measurements.

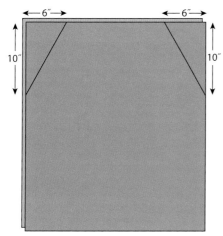

Measure top corners and mark.

3 Press under ½″ along the bottom edges of both fabrics.

4 Cut on the two diagonal lines. Sew the sides and top of the apron together, leaving the bottom open.

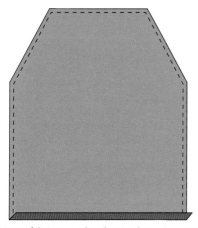

Sew 2 fabrics together, leaving bottom open.

5 Clip the fabric corners at the top. Turn the apron right side out. Press.

SEW THE CHANNELS FOR THE RIBBON

1 Press under 1¼″ along the 2 diagonal edges to create channels for the ribbon ties. Pin in place.

2 Sewing from the back of the apron, sew very close to the edge on both sides of the diagonal channels. Leave the ends of each channel open.

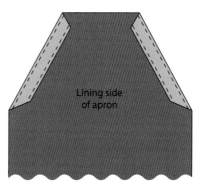

Stitch channels for ribbon ties.

ATTACH THE POCKET TO THE APRON

1 Place the pocket 11″ down from the top of the apron and 4″ from each side edge. Pin in place. Topstitch all the way around the pocket, leaving the top open.

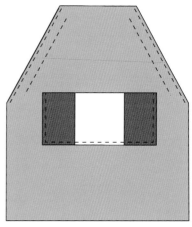

Stitch pocket to apron.

2 Topstitch in the ditch between the paper-pieced block and each side rectangle, if desired, to create sections in the pocket.

CONSTRUCT THE RUFFLE

1 Fold the Fabric B 9″ × WOF strip in half lengthwise with right sides together and pin. Sew the 2 short sides and backtack.

Fold and stitch ruffle piece.

2 Turn the ruffle right side out and press. Gather the long open edge of the ruffle. (I use dental tape to gather fabric. I zigzag over the dental tape and pull on it to gather the fabric.) Gather the ruffle to fit inside the bottom opening in the apron and pin in place.

3 Topstitch ¼″ from the bottom of the apron piece to encase the ruffle.

Stitch gathered ruffle to bottom of apron.

FINISHING

1 Thread the 4 yard piece of ribbon through the channels in the apron. Try on the apron for fit. Trim any excess ribbon and knot each end.

Pillow

FINISHED PILLOW: 17˝ × 14˝

Materials

Fabric A: ¾ yard for sashing and pillow back

Fabric B: 1 rectangle 14½″ × 17½″ for backing for quilting (muslin recommended)

Assorted scraps: For paper piecing block (*See your selected block's materials list.*)

Fusible Batting: 1 rectangle 14½″ × 17½″

Pillow form 12″ × 16″

Cutting

Yardages are based on 42″ usable width of fabric (WOF). Fold fabric selvage to selvage.

Fabric A

• Cut 1 strip 1½″ × WOF.

• Subcut 2 strips 1½″ × 8″.

• Cut 1 strip 3¾″ × WOF.

• Subcut 2 strips 3¾″ × 17½″.

• Cut 1 strip 14½″ × WOF.

• Subcut into 2 rectangles 14½″ × 12″.

Sewing

Use ¼″ seams throughout unless otherwise directed.

PAPER-PIECED BLOCK

Refer to Paper-Piecing Basics (page 7) as needed.

1. Paper piece 1 rectangular block, of your choosing (from Pattern Blocks, pages 52–78), using the assorted scraps. (*See your selected block's materials list.*)

2. Add any necessary embroidery.

3. Trim the block to 8″ × 15½″.

ATTACH THE SASHING TO THE BLOCK

1 Sew a Fabric A 1½″ × 8″ strip to the sides of the rectangular block. Press the seams toward the sashing.

Sew strips to sides of block.

2 Sew a Fabric A 3¾″ × 17½″ strip to the top and bottom of the block. Press the seams toward the sashing.

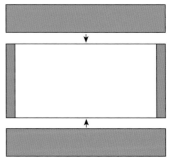

Sew strips to top and bottom of block.

QUILT

1 Remove the paper from the back of the block.

2 Steam press the fusible batting to the back of the paper-pieced unit. Pin the Fabric B backing (right side facing down) and quilt top (right side facing up).

3 Quilt as desired.

PREPARE THE PILLOW BACK

1 Press under ½″ along one 14½″ edge of each of the Fabric A pillow back pieces. Turn under another ½″ and press again.

2 Stitch the hem in place, stitching close to the pressed edge.

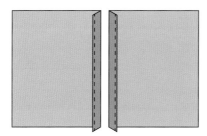

Stitch hem on pillow back pieces.

3 Arrange the 2 pillow back pieces, right side up, overlapping each other about 4″.

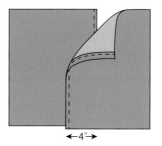

←—4″—→

Overlap pillow back pieces.

4 With right sides together, pin the pillow front to the pillow backs, adjusting the back pieces to fit. Stitch all the way around. Turn the pillow right side out. Gently poke out the corners to make them square. Press.

5 Topstitch 1″ from the edges of the pillow.

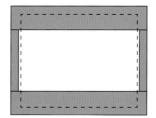

6 Place the pillow form into the pillow.

Table Runner

FINISHED TABLE RUNNER: 15″ × 33¾″

Materials

Fabric A: ¼ yard each of 5 coordinating fabrics for pinwheel blocks and squares

Fabric B: ¼ yard of contrasting fabric for pinwheel blocks

Fabric C: ⅔ yard for backing

Fabric D: ⅓ yard for binding

Fabric E: ½ yard for background for paper-pieced blocks

Assorted scraps: For paper piecing blocks (*See your selected block's materials list.*)

Batting: 1 rectangle 21″ × 40″

Cutting

Yardages are based on 42″ usable width of fabric (WOF). Fold fabric selvage to selvage.

Fabric A

- Cut 1 strip 4¼″ × WOF from each of the 5 fabrics. Subcut into a total of 20 squares 4¼″ × 4¼″.

Fabric B

- Cut 1 strip 4¼″ × WOF. Subcut into 7 squares 4¼″ × 4¼″.

Fabric D

- Cut 3 strips 2½″ × WOF for binding.

Sewing

Use ¼″ seams throughout unless otherwise directed.

PAPER-PIECED BLOCKS

Refer to Paper-Piecing Basics (page 7) as needed.

1 Paper piece 2 rectangular blocks of your choosing (from Pattern Blocks, pages 52–78), using Fabric E for the background and the assorted fabrics for the rest of each block. (*See your selected block's materials list.*)

2 Add any necessary embroidery.

3 Trim each block to 8″ × 15½″.

CREATE THE PINWHEEL BLOCKS

1 Pin a Fabric A 4¼″ × 4¼″ square on top of a Fabric B 4¼″ × 4¼″ square, right sides together. Sew a ¼″ seam on the outer edges.

Sew 2 squares together.

2 Cut the sewn squares diagonally in both directions to make 4 half-square triangle pieces.

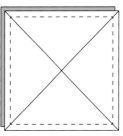

Cut squares diagonally.

3 Open the 4 pieces and press the seams toward the darker fabric.

4 Arrange the pieces to form the pinwheel block.

5 Sew the adjoining sides of Pieces 1 and 2 and Pieces 3 and 4 together. Press the seams open.

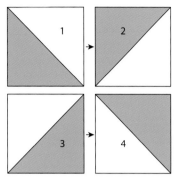

Sew pieces into sections.

6 Sew Sections 1 and 2 to Sections 3 and 4. Press the seams open.

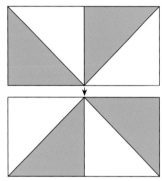

Sew sections together.

7 Repeat Steps 1–6 to make the remaining pinwheel blocks. Trim the 7 finished pinwheel blocks to 4¼" × 4¼", if they are not already at that size.

ASSEMBLE THE BLOCKS AND SQUARES

1 Sew the pinwheel blocks to the remaining Fabric A squares. Create 1 row with 2 pinwheel blocks and 2 squares.

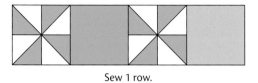

Sew 1 row.

2 Create 3 rows with 1 pinwheel block and 3 squares.

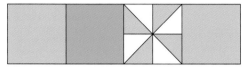

Sew 3 rows.

3 Create 1 row with 2 pinwheel blocks and 2 squares.

Sew 1 row.

4 Arrange and sew the 5 rows together, turning the rows as shown. Press the seams up.

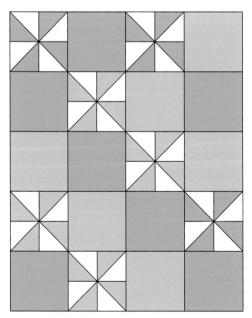

Finished layout for assembled rows

ASSEMBLE THE TABLE RUNNER

1 Sew the top edge of each rectangular paper-pieced block to the top and bottom edges of the joined rows so they mirror each other.

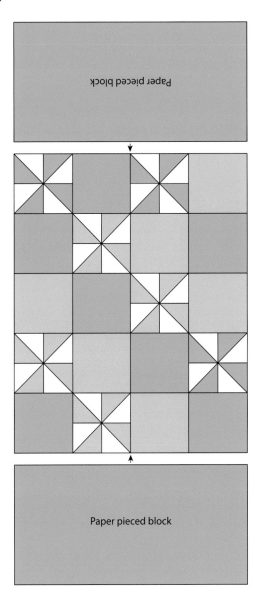

Attach paper-pieced blocks.

QUILTING

1 Remove the paper from the back of the blocks.

2 Layer the Fabric C backing (right side facing down), batting, and table runner top (right side facing up).

3 Pin all 3 layers together and quilt as desired.

BINDING

Follow the instructions in Lap Quilt, Binding (page 15), using the Fabric D 2½″ × WOF strips.

Stockings

Cat Stocking

FINISHED STOCKING: 9½″ wide x 18″ long

Here's a Christmas stocking for your favorite kitty. Meow!

Materials

Fabric A: ¾ yard for stocking front and back (I used prequilted fabric.)

Fabric B: ¾ yard for lining

Assorted scraps: For paper piecing blocks (*See your selected block's materials list.*)

Fusible batting: 1 square 8″ × 8″

HeatnBond Lite: Scraps

Ribbon: 13″ piece 1″ wide grosgrain

Cutting

Yardages are based on 42″ usable width of fabric (WOF). Fold fabric selvage to selvage.

Fabric A

- Cut 1 stocking front bottom piece using the Cat Paw Template (page 38).

- Cut 1 square 8″ × 8″ for the stocking front top piece.

- After completing Assemble the Stocking Front (pages 35–36), use the assembled stocking front to cut 1 complete stocking back.

Fabric B

- Using the assembled stocking front, cut 2 complete stocking linings.

Sewing

Use ¼″ seams throughout unless otherwise directed.

PAPER-PIECED BLOCK

Refer to Paper-Piecing Basics (page 7) as needed.

1 Paper piece 1 square block of your choosing (from Pattern Blocks, pages 52–78), using the assorted scraps. (*See your selected block's materials list.*)

2 Add any necessary embroidery.

3 Trim the block to 8″ × 8″.

QUILT THE BLOCK

1 Remove the paper from the back of the paper-pieced block.

2 Steam press the fusible batting to the back of the paper-pieced block.

3 Quilt as desired.

ASSEMBLE THE STOCKING FRONT

1 Follow the manufacturer's instructions to fuse the paw details to the Cat Paw piece, using HeatnBond Lite and Fabric B scraps. Satin stitch around the edges of the appliqué pieces.

2 Sew the stocking front 8″ × 8″ square to the top of the paper-pieced block, right sides together. Press the seam toward the block. Sew the appliquéd Cat Paw piece to the bottom of the block. Press the seam toward the block.

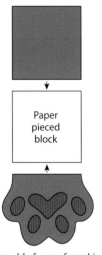

Assemble front of stocking.

3 Use the assembled stocking front to cut out 1 stocking back piece from Fabric A and 2 stocking lining pieces from Fabric B.

PERSONALIZE THE LINING

1 If desired, machine embroider a name at the top of one of the Fabric B lining pieces. The letters should start 1½″ down from the top of the lining and must be positioned so they are upside down when the Cat Paw is at the bottom. Letters can be

approximately 1½″ high. I used the *Cutie Patootie* font.

Lettering is embroidered at top of lining.

ASSEMBLE THE STOCKING WITH THE LINING

1 Sew the personalized piece of lining to the top of the stocking front, right sides together.

Sew lining to stocking.

2 Repeat Step 1 with the remaining piece of lining and the stocking back.

3 Pin the 2 sections of the stocking together, with right sides of the same fabrics together.

4 Sew all the way around the stocking and lining, leaving a 7″ opening in one side of the lining.

Sew, leaving opening.

5 Clip the curves. Turn the stocking right side out. Hand stitch to close the opening. Push the lining into the stocking. Press.

RIBBON HANGER

 Fold the 13″ piece of grosgrain ribbon in half and sew the ends together.

Sew ends of ribbon hanger together.

2 Pin the ribbon hanger 4½″ down from the top of the stocking and sew through all thicknesses. Using the arm of the sewing machine works great!

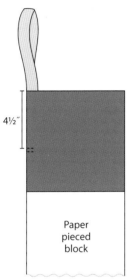

4½″

Paper pieced block

Sew hanger to stocking.

3 Fold down the stocking top to show the embroidered name.

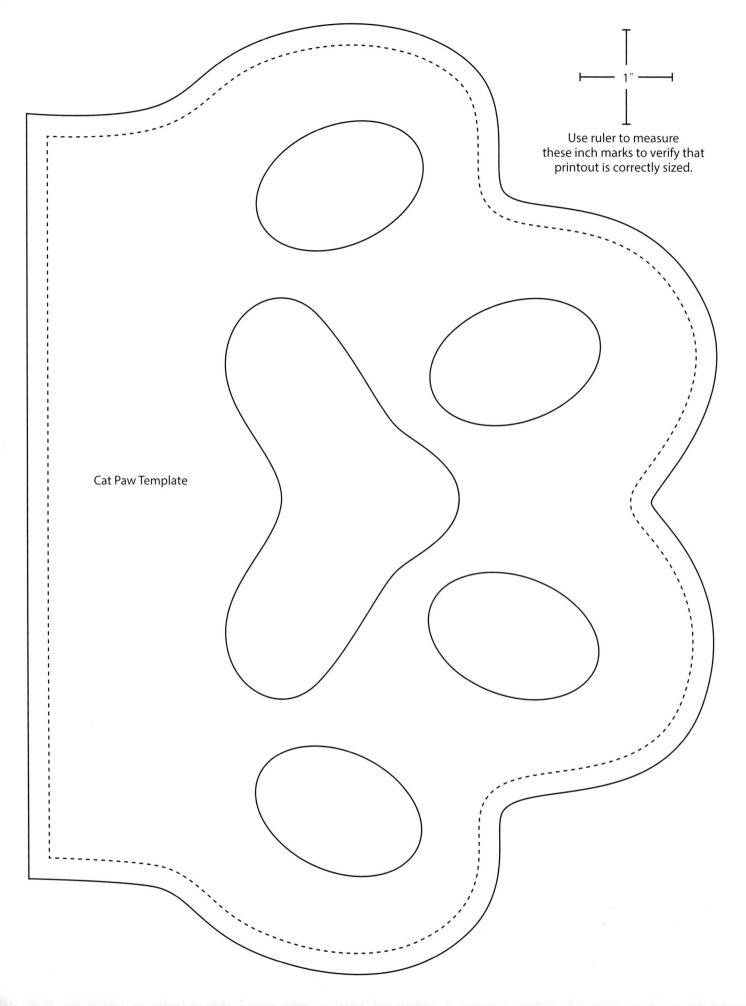

1″

Use ruler to measure
these inch marks to verify that
printout is correctly sized.

Cat Paw Template

Dog Stocking

FINISHED STOCKING: 10½˝ wide x 20˝ long

This Christmas stocking is for the puppy in your life. Woof!

Materials

Fabric A: ¾ yard for main fabric (I used prequilted fabric.)

Fabric B: ¾ yard for lining

Assorted scraps: For paper piecing blocks (*See your selected block's materials list.*)

Fusible batting: 1 square 8˝ × 8˝

Ribbon: 10˝ piece 1˝ wide grosgrain

Rickrack: 20˝ piece 1¼˝ wide (optional)

Cutting

Yardages are based on 42˝ usable width of fabric (WOF). Fold fabric selvage to selvage.

Fabric A

- Cut 2 stocking end pieces using the Dog Bone Template (page 42).

- After completing Assemble the Stocking Front (page 40), use the assembled stocking front to cut 1 complete stocking back.

Fabric B

- Using the assembled stocking front, cut 2 complete stocking linings.

Sewing

Use ¼˝ seams throughout unless otherwise directed.

PAPER-PIECED BLOCK

Refer to Paper-Piecing Basics (page 7) as needed.

1 Paper piece 1 square block of your choosing (from Pattern Blocks, pages 52–78), using the assorted scraps. (*See your selected block's materials list.*)

2 Add any necessary embroidery.

3 Trim the block to 8˝ × 8˝.

QUILT THE BLOCK

1 Remove the paper from the back of the paper-pieced block.

2 Steam press the fusible batting to the back of the paper-pieced block.

3 Quilt as desired.

ASSEMBLE THE STOCKING FRONT

1 Sew a Dog Bone end piece to the top and bottom of the paper-pieced block, right sides together. Press the seams toward the block.

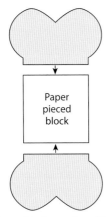

Assemble front of stocking.

2 Use the assembled stocking front to cut out 1 stocking back piece from Fabric A and 2 stocking lining pieces from Fabric B.

PERSONALIZE THE FRONT OF THE STOCKING

1 If desired, machine embroider a name at the top of one of the end pieces. The letters should be centered on the Dog Bone. Letters can be approximately 1½″ high. I used the *Cutie Patootie* font.

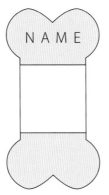

Lettering embroidered on top piece

2 If desired, sew a 10″ length of rickrack next to the seams of the paper-pieced block.

Sew rickrack at seams.

3 Trim the rickrack ends even with the stocking edges.

ATTACH THE LINING TO THE STOCKING

1 Fold the 10″ piece of grosgrain ribbon in half and pin the raw edges to the seamline of the stocking front, as indicated by the dot on the template (page 42).

Pin ribbon in place.

2 With right sides together, sew the lining to the stocking piece along the top from dot to dot, backtacking at the dots.

Sew lining to stocking piece at top only.

3 Repeat Step 2, using the remaining piece of lining and the stocking back.

4 Clip the curves and turn the pieces right side out. Press along the top of each assembled piece. At this point, the stocking pieces are only sewn to each piece of lining along the top edge.

ASSEMBLE THE STOCKING

1 Pin the front and back sections of the stocking, right sides together.

2 Pin the front and back sections of the lining, right sides together. Leave the sewn top sections unpinned.

3 Sew all the way around the stocking and lining pieces, leaving a 7″ opening in one side of the lining. Make sure to catch the raw ends of the rickrack in the seams.

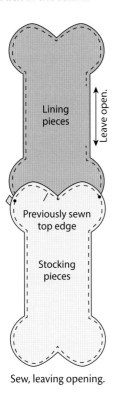

Sew, leaving opening.

4 Turn the stocking right side out through the opening. Hand stitch to close the opening. Push the lining into the stocking. Press.

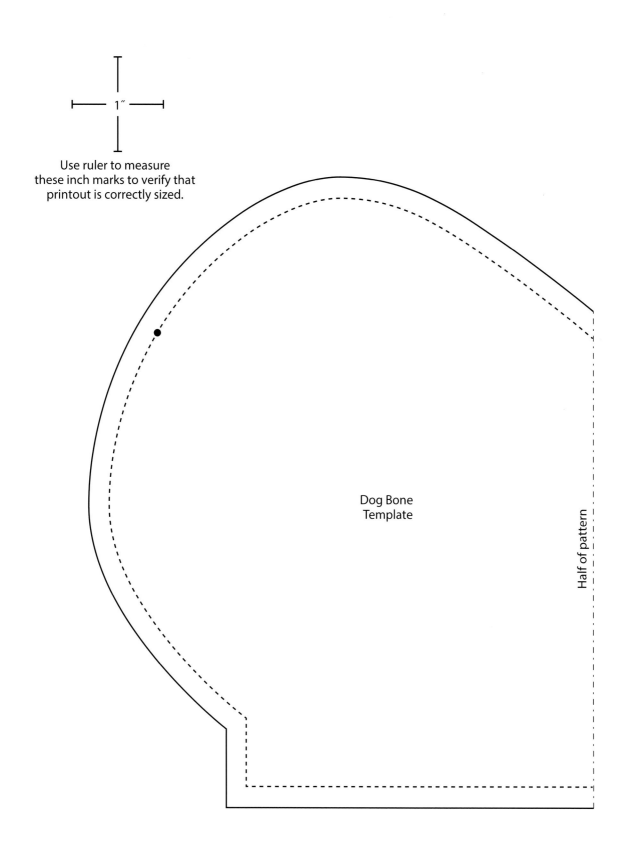

1″

Use ruler to measure
these inch marks to verify that
printout is correctly sized.

Dog Bone
Template

Half of pattern

Zippy Pouch

FINISHED POUCH: 11˝ wide x 9˝ long x 4˝ deep

Materials

Fabric A: ½ yard for main fabric

Fabric B: ½ yard for lining

Fabric C: 2 scraps 2″ × 2″ for tabs

Assorted scraps: For paper piecing blocks *(See your selected block's materials list.)*

Fusible T-shirt quilt interfacing: 12″ × 12″ piece (such as Stabili-TEE Fusible Interfacing by C&T Publishing)

Zipper: 12″ or longer (polyester)

Cutting

Yardages are based on 42″ usable width of fabric (WOF). Fold fabric selvage to selvage.

Fabric A

Cut 1 strip 2½″ × WOF.

• Subcut into 2 strips 2½″ × 8″ and 2 strips 2½″ × 12″.

• Cut 1 square 12″ × 12″.

Fabric B

• Cut 2 squares 12″ × 12″.

Sewing

Use ¼″ seams throughout unless otherwise directed.

PAPER-PIECED BLOCK

Refer to Paper-Piecing Basics (page 7) as needed.

1 Paper piece 1 square block of your choosing (from Pattern Blocks, pages 52–78), following the fabric guide for the block. *(See your selected block's materials list.)*

2 Add any necessary embroidery.

3 Trim the block to 8″ × 8″.

ASSEMBLE THE FRONT OF THE POUCH

1 Sew a Fabric A 2½″ × 8″ strip to the top and bottom of the paper-pieced block. Press the seams toward the block.

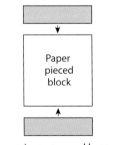

Sew strips to top and bottom.

2 Sew a Fabric A 2½″ × 12″ strip to the sides of the paper-pieced block. Press the seams toward the block.

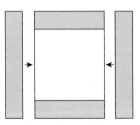

Sew strips to sides.

3 Remove the paper from the back of the paper-pieced block. Steam press the fusible T-shirt quilt interfacing to the back of the block.

4 Quilt the block as desired.

PREPARE THE ZIPPER

1 Trim the zipper to 11″ to make it 1″ shorter than the fabric pieces.

Trim zipper.

2 Create zipper tabs with the Fabric C 2″ × 2″ squares by folding each square in half. Press, then fold the side edges in to the center crease and press again.

Press 2 tabs.

3 Position a tab on each end of the zipper and stitch in place close to the open edges of the tab.

Sew tabs to zipper ends.

ATTACH THE ZIPPER TO THE POUCH

1 Note: Use a zipper foot for these steps. Sew the zipper to the top of the paper-pieced unit, right sides together. Press the seam toward the fabric.

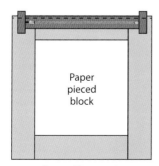

Sew front of bag to zipper.

2 Place the Fabric A square over the zipper, right sides together, and stitch along the other edge of the zipper. Press the seam toward the fabric.

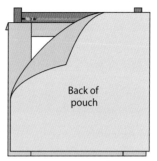

Stitch second edge of zipper.

3 Place 1 of the Fabric B lining pieces over the top of the zipper tape, with the right side of the lining facing the wrong side of the zipper. Stitch in place.

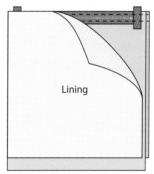

Sew first piece of lining over zipper.

4 Flip the first piece of lining out of the way, gently pressing the fabric flat.

5 Repeat Steps 3 and 4 with the second piece of lining, stitching it to the opposite edge of the zipper.

6 Flip the second piece of lining out of the way and gently press it in place.

ASSEMBLE THE POUCH

1 Mark and cut a 2″ × 2″ square from the bottom corners of each pouch piece and each lining piece.

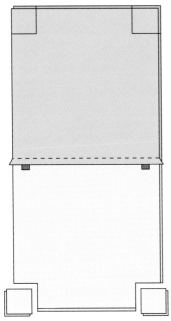

Cut squares from bottom corners.

2 Unzip the zipper three-fourths of the way open. Pin the 2 pouch pieces, right sides together. Pin the 2 lining pieces, right sides together. Squish and pinch the zipper tabs toward the lining side. Sew the side and bottom edges together, leaving a 5″ opening on one lining piece side. Do not stitch the cut corners.

Leave open.

Pin together and sew.

3 To make the boxed corners, match each side seam with the adjacent bottom seam. Flatten and align the raw edges. Pin and sew together. Repeat for each of the pouch and lining corners.

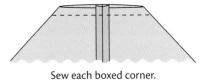

Sew each boxed corner.

4 Turn the pouch right side out through the lining opening. Push the lining into the inside of the pouch. Hand stitch to close the opening.

5 Topstitch ¼″ away from the zipper on each side, if desired, starting and stopping 1″ from each end.

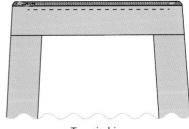

Topstitching

Gift Bag

Materials

Fabric A: Fat quarter (18″ × 20″) for front top and back

Fabric B: ⅛ yard for drawstring

Fabric C: Fat quarter (18″ × 20″) for lining

Fusible T-shirt interfacing: 8″ × 8″ square (Stabili-TEE Fusible Interfacing by C&T Publishing recommended)

Assorted scraps: For paper piecing (*See your selected block's materials list.*)

Cutting

Yardages are based on 42″ usable width of fabric (WOF). Fold fabric selvage to selvage.

Fabric A

• Cut 1 rectangle 8″ × 6″ and 1 rectangle 8″ × 13½″.

Fabric B

• Cut 1 strip 2″ × WOF.

Fabric C

• Cut 1 rectangle 8″ × 19″.

Sewing

Use ¼″ seams throughout unless otherwise directed.

PAPER-PIECED BLOCK

Refer to Paper-Piecing Basics (page 7) as needed.

1 Paper piece 1 square block of your choosing (from Pattern Blocks, pages 52–78), using the assorted scraps. (*See your selected block's materials list.*)

2 Add any necessary embroidery.

3 Trim the block to 8″ × 8″.

CONSTRUCT THE OUTSIDE OF THE BAG

1 Sew the Fabric A 8″ × 6″ rectangle to the top of the paper-pieced block. Press the seam toward the rectangle.

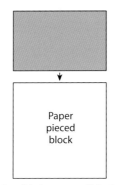

Sew fabric to top of block.

2 With right sides together, sew the Fabric A 13½″ × 8″ back rectangle to the bag front. Stop sewing and backtack 1″ above the paper-pieced block seam on one side. Leave the rest of the side and the top of the bag open.

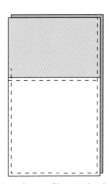

Sew front of bag to back.

3 Press under ¼″ on the open side seam edges. Stitch in place.

4 Press under ½″ to the wrong side along the open top edge of the bag.

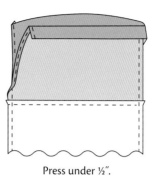

Hem side edges of bag.

Press under ½″.

CONSTRUCT THE BAG LINING

1 Fold the Fabric C 8″ × 19″ lining piece in half, right sides together. Sew the side seams. Turn right side out.

2 Push the bag inside the lining, wrong sides together. Fold the top of the bag to overlap the raw edge of the lining ½″. Pin in place and press along the top folded edge of the bag. Sew the bag to the lining, stitching ⅛″ from the overlapped edge.

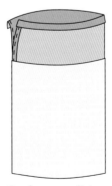

Sew bag top to lining.

3 Sew 1″ above the previous stitching to create the channel for the drawstring. Backtack at the beginning and end of the stitching.

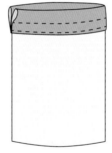

Sew channel for drawstring.

CONSTRUCT THE DRAWSTRING

1 Press the Fabric B 2″ × WOF drawstring strip in half lengthwise. Fold the raw sides of the strip into the center fold and press again, creating a strip that is ½″ wide.

Press drawstring to ½″ wide.

2 Stitch along the long folded edge of the drawstring.

3 Using a safety pin or bodkin, feed the drawstring into the 1″ channel on the bag. Trim the ends of the drawstring to 12″ long, cutting the remainder off at a diagonal. Tie a knot on each end of the drawstring.

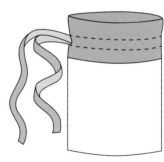

Feed drawstring through channel.

Block Patterns

Refer to Paper-Piecing Basics (page 7) as needed when making the blocks.

• Refer to the specific project instructions about when to remove foundation papers.

• Any hand embroidery included in the following block instructions is meant to be done with foundation papers attached.

• For hand embroidery, I use a running stitch or make French knots using 6 strands of embroidery floss.

• The first fabric in the materials list is for the block background. If your project includes background fabric in its materials list, you can ignore the background fabric listed for the block.

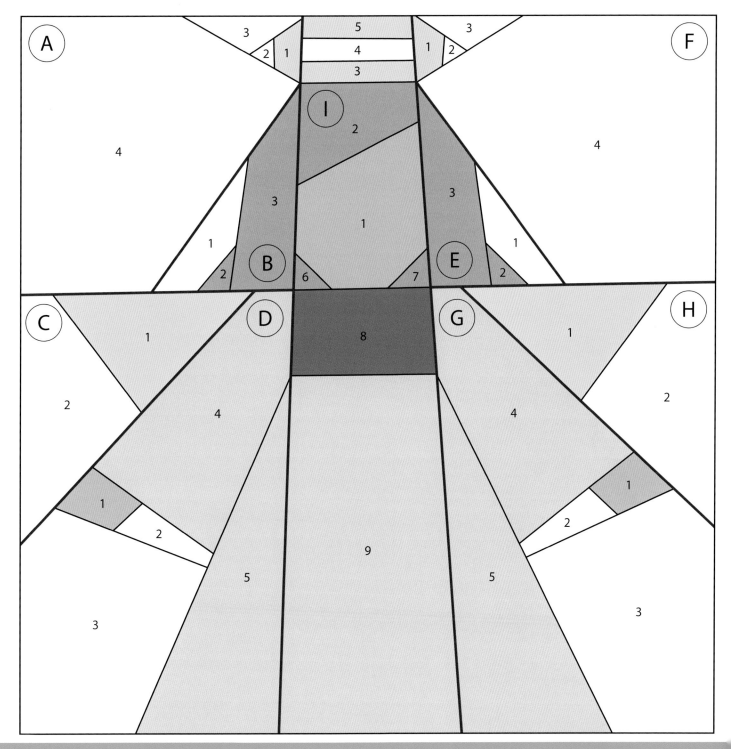

ANGEL

Materials
- **Scraps:** White, at least 9″ × 11″; blue; blue satin; peach; brown; metallic gold

Directions
For detailed directions, refer to Paper-Piecing Basics (page 7).

1. Make 3 copies of the pattern (A/D/E, B/F/G, C/H/I).

2. Cut around each segment, adding ¼″ seam allowances.

3. Paper piece each segment.

4. Connect the segments: A to B; C to D; A/B to C/D; E to F; G to H; E/F to G/H; A–D to I to E–H.

5. Trim the block to 8″ × 8″.

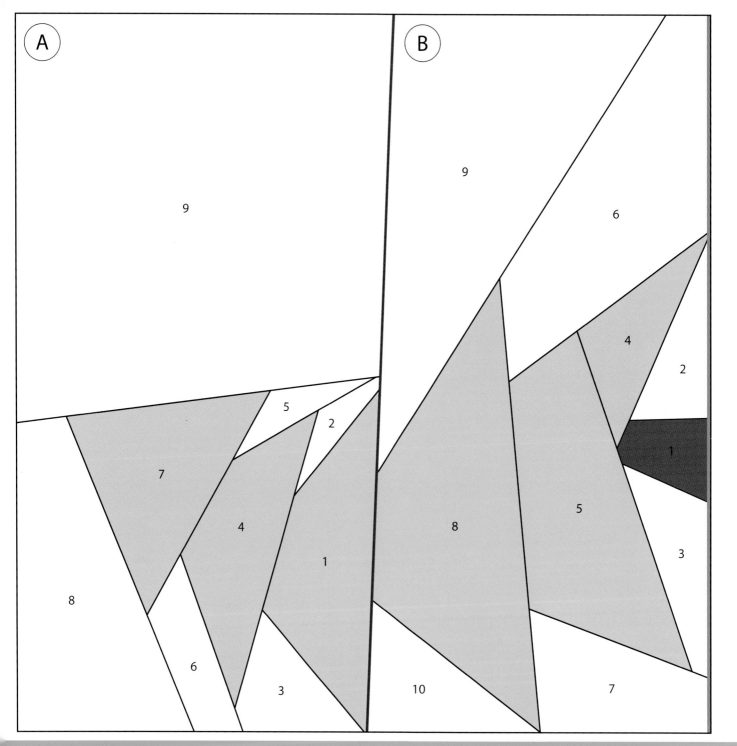

BEAR WITH TREE, PART 1

Materials

• **Scraps:** White, at least 9″ × 11″; dark brown; green

Directions

For detailed directions, refer to Paper-Piecing Basics (page 7).

1. Make 2 copies of the pattern (A, B).

2. Cut around each segment, adding ¼″ seam allowances.

3. Paper piece each segment.

4. Connect the segments: A to B.

5. Trim ¼″ from the blue line.

6. Continue to Bear with Tree, Part 2 (next page).

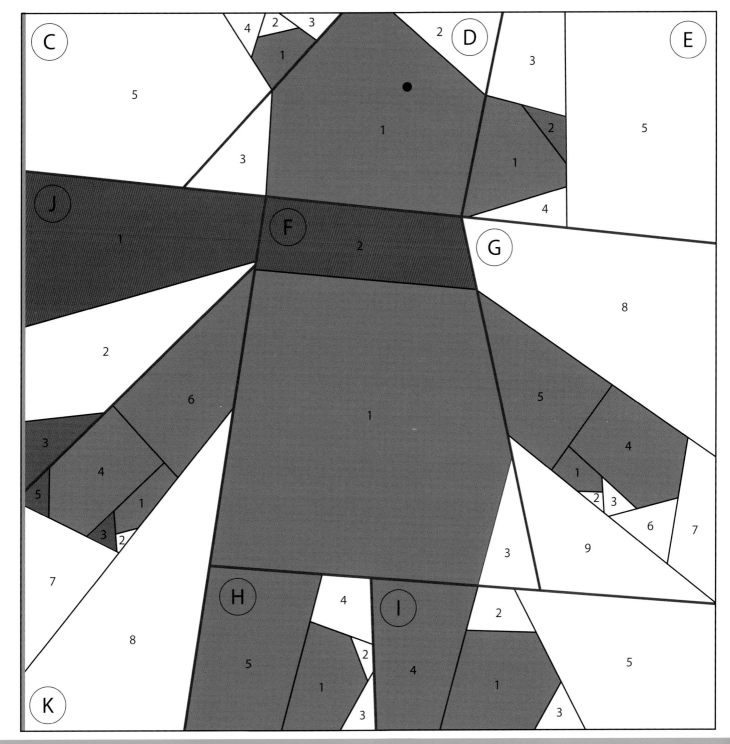

BEAR WITH TREE, PART 2

Materials

- **Scraps:** White, at least 9″ × 11″; dark brown; light brown; red; black

- **Embroidery floss:** Black

Directions

For detailed directions, refer to Paper-Piecing Basics (page 7).

1. Make 4 copies of the pattern (C/E/I/K, D/H, F, G/J).

2. Cut around each segment, adding ¼″ seam allowances.

3. Paper piece each segment.

4. Connect the segments: C to D to E; F to G; H to I; F/G to H/I; J to K; F–I to J/K; C/D/E to F–K.

5. Trim ¼″ from the blue line. Match and sew Part 1 to Part 2 on the blue lines.

6. Trim the block to 8″ × 15 ½″.

7. Hand stitch a French knot for the eye with black embroidery floss.

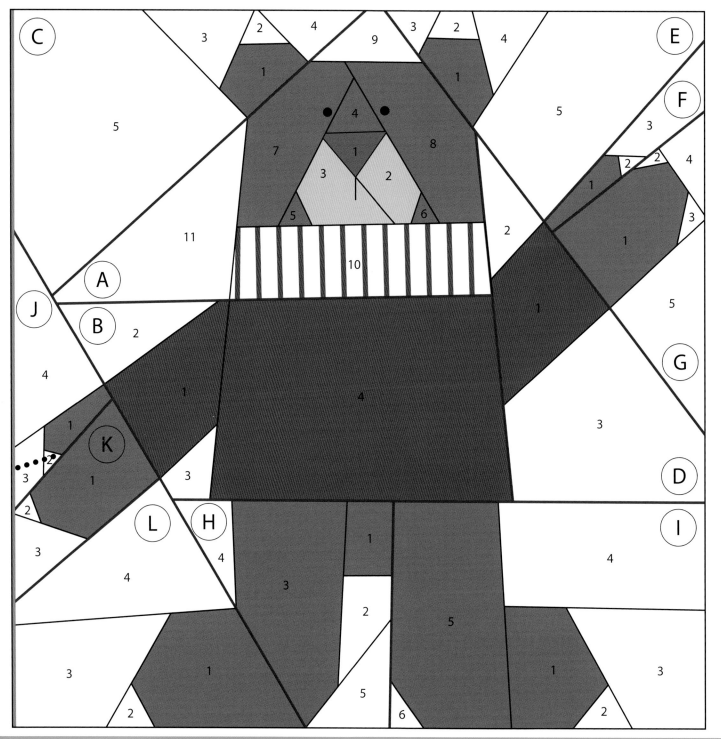

Materials
- **Scraps:** White, at least 9″ × 11″; brown; tan; red stripe; dark red; black
- **Embroidery floss:** Black

Directions
For detailed directions, refer to Paper-Piecing Basics (page 7).

1. Make 4 copies of the pattern (A/F/I/K, B/E, C/G/H, D/J/L).

2. Cut around each segment, adding ¼″ seam allowances.

3. Paper piece each segment.

4. Connect the segments: A to B to C to D; E to F to G; A–D to E/F/G; H to I; A–G to H/I; J to K to L; A–I to J/K/L.

5. Trim ¼″ from the blue line.

6. Using black embroidery floss, hand stitch the mouth and rope and embroider French knots for the eyes.

7. Continue to Bear-ing Gifts, Part 2 (next page).

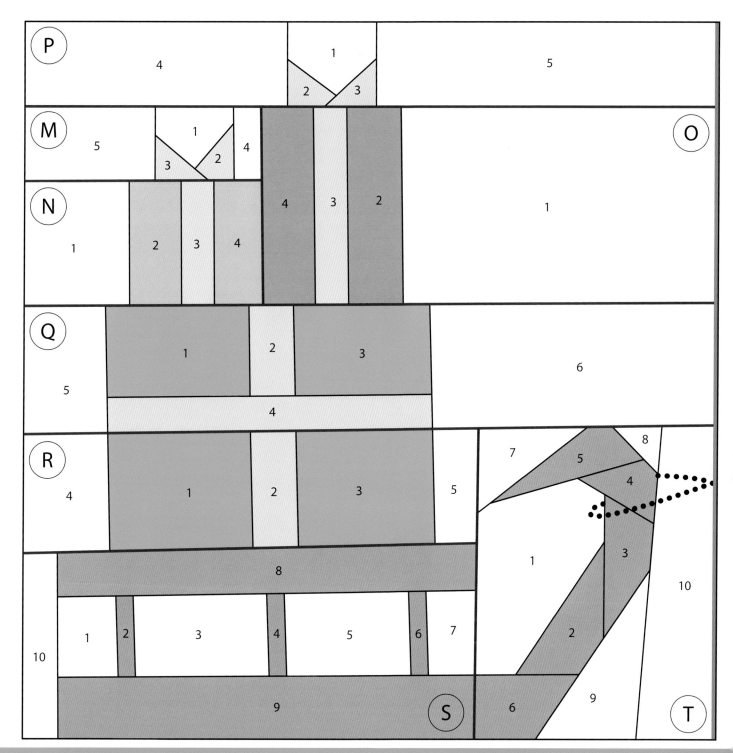

BEAR-ING GIFTS, PART 2

Materials

- **Scraps:** White, at least 9″ × 11″; brown; red; green; turquoise; gold
- **Embroidery floss:** Black

Directions

For detailed directions, refer to Paper-Piecing Basics (page 7).

1. Make 3 copies of the pattern (M/Q/S, N/P/R, O/T).

2. Cut around each segment, adding ¼″ seam allowances.

3. Paper piece each segment.

4. Connect the segments: M to N; M/N to O; M/N/O to P to Q; R to S; R/S to T; M–Q to R/S/T.

5. Trim ¼″ from the blue line. Match and sew Part 1 to Part 2 on the blue lines.

6. Trim the block to 8″ × 15½″.

7. Hand stitch the rope with black embroidery floss.

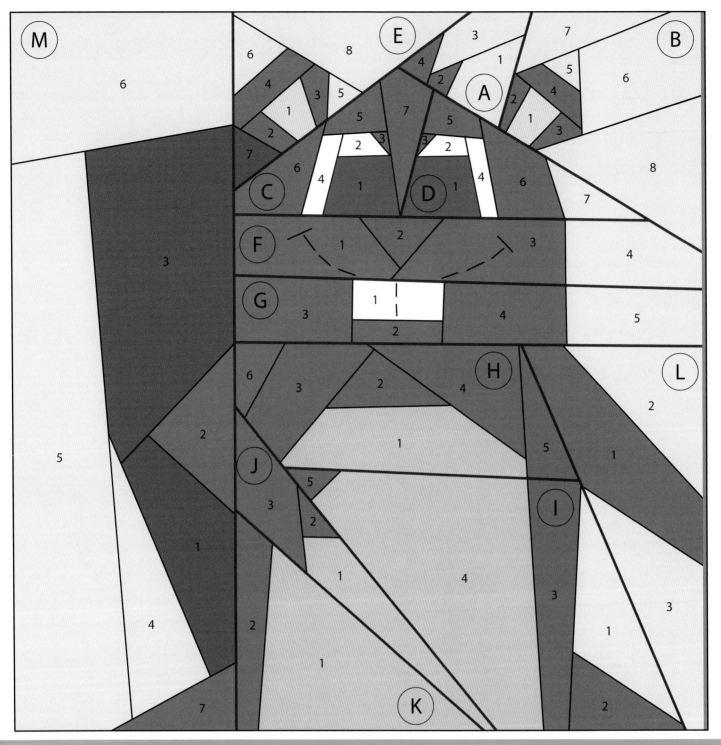

BEAVER EATING TREE, PART 1

Materials

- **Scraps:** Turquoise, at least 9″ × 11″; black; light brown; red-brown; dark brown; tan; white
- **Embroidery floss:** Black

Directions

For detailed directions, refer to Paper-Piecing Basics (page 7).

1. Make 4 copies of the pattern (A/F/H/K, B/C/G/J, D/E/I, L/M).

2. Cut around each segment, adding ¼″ seam allowances.

3. Paper piece each segment.

4. Connect the segments: A to B; C to D; F to G; C/D to F/G to A/B to E; H to I; H/I to J to K to L; A–G to H–L; A–L to M.

5. Trim ¼″ from the blue line.

6. Hand stitch the tooth and mouth with black embroidery floss.

7. Continue to Beaver Eating Tree, Part 2 (next page).

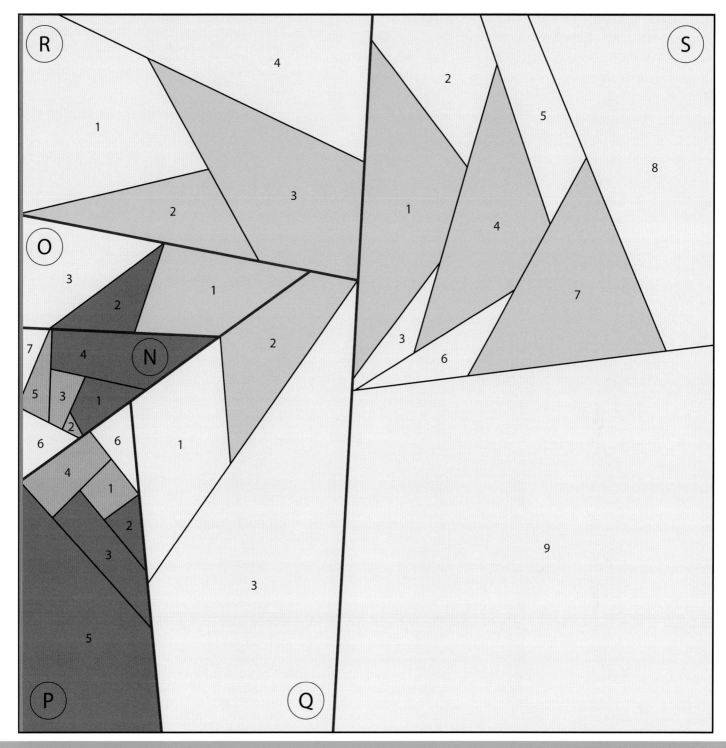

BEAVER EATING TREE, PART 2

Materials
- **Scraps:** Turquoise, at least 9″ × 11″; dark brown; tan; green

Directions

For detailed directions, refer to Paper-Piecing Basics (page 7).

1. Make 3 copies of the pattern (N/R, O/P/S, Q).

2. Cut around each segment, adding ¼″ seam allowances.

3. Paper piece each segment.

4. Connect the segments: N to O; P to Q; N/O to P/Q to R; N–R to S.

5. Trim ¼″ from the blue line. Match and sew Part 1 to Part 2 on the blue lines.

6. Trim the block to 8″ × 15½″.

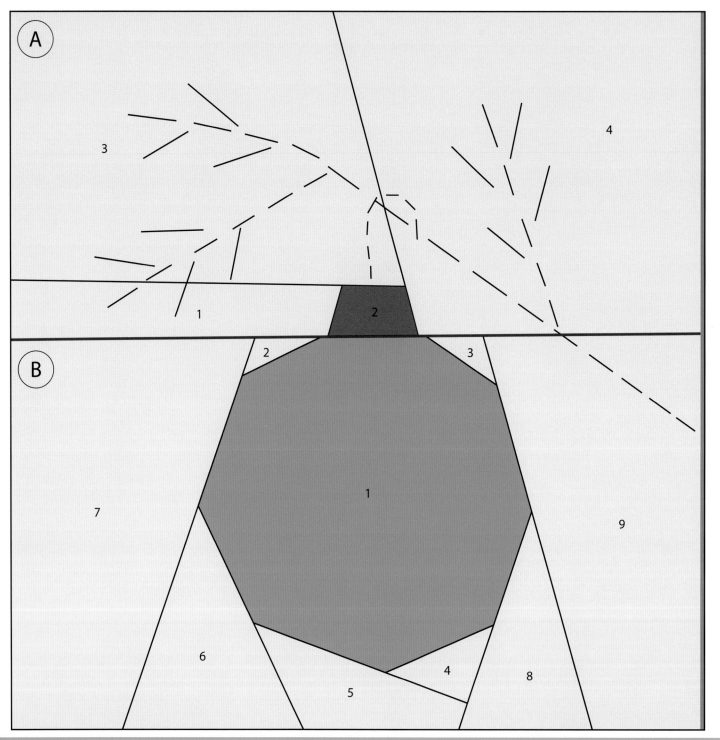

BUNNY WITH ORNAMENT, PART 1

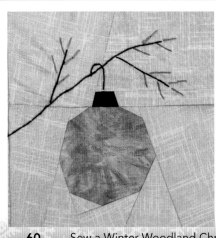

Materials

- **Scraps:** Turquoise, at least 9″ × 11″; black; teal
- **Embroidery floss:** Black, green

Directions

For detailed directions, refer to Paper-Piecing Basics (page 7).

1. Make 2 copies of the pattern (A, B).

2. Cut around each segment, adding ¼″ seam allowances.

3. Paper piece each segment.

4. Connect the segments: A to B.

5. Trim ¼″ from the blue line.

6. Continue to Bunny, Part 2 (next page).

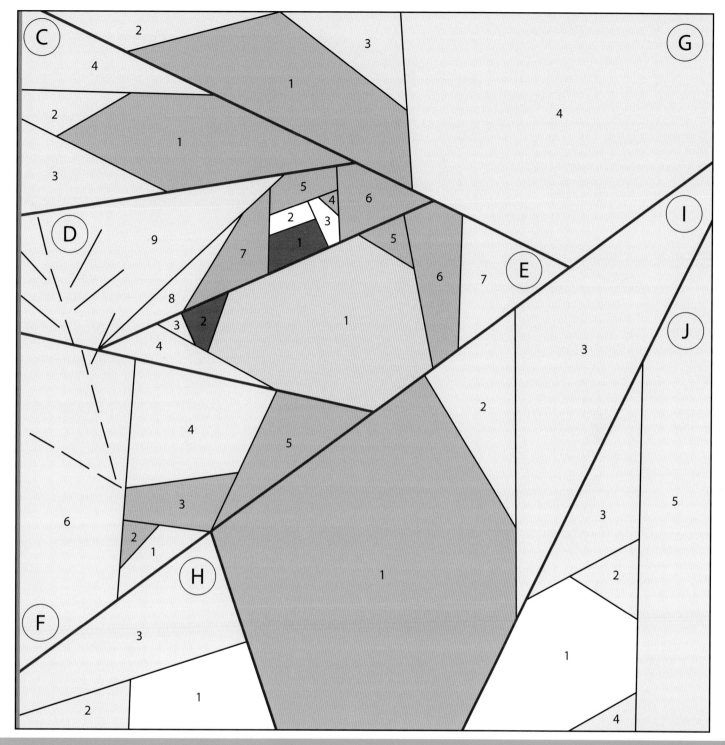

BUNNY WITH ORNAMENT, PART 2

Materials

- **Scraps:** Turquoise, at least 9″ × 11″; gray; black; white; pink

- **Embroidery floss:** Black

Directions

For detailed directions, refer to Paper-Piecing Basics (page 7).

1. Make 3 copies of the pattern (C/E/H/J, D/I, F/G).

2. Cut around each segment, adding ¼″ seam allowances.

3. Paper piece each segment.

4. Connect the segments: C to D to E; C/D/E to F to G; H to I to J; C–G to H/I/J.

5. Trim ¼″ from the blue line. Match and sew Part 1 to Part 2 on the blue lines.

6. Trim the block to 8″ × 15½″.

7. Hand stitch the branch with black embroidery floss and the needles with green embroidery floss.

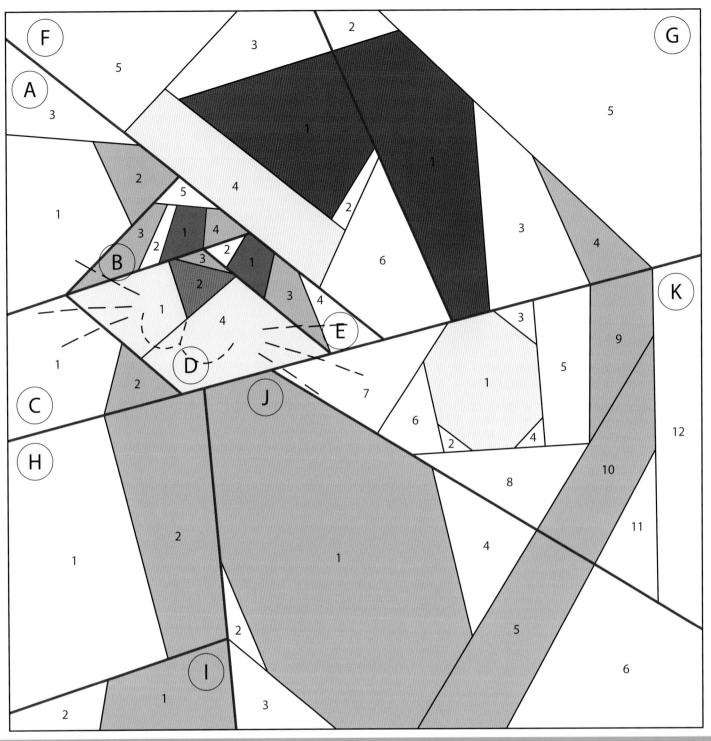

CAT

Materials

- **Scraps:** White, at least 9″ × 11″; medium gray; light gray; pink; red; dark red; white; black
- **Embroidery floss:** Black

Directions

For detailed directions, refer to Paper-Piecing Basics (page 7).

1. Make 5 copies of the pattern (A/G/H, B/J, C/E/I, D/F, K).

2. Cut around each segment, adding ¼″ seam allowances.

3. Paper piece each segment.

4. Connect the segments: A to B; C to D to E; A/B to C/D/E; A–E to F to G; H to I; H/I to J to K; A–G to H–K.

5. Trim the block to 8″ × 8″.

6. Hand stitch the mouth and whiskers with black embroidery floss.

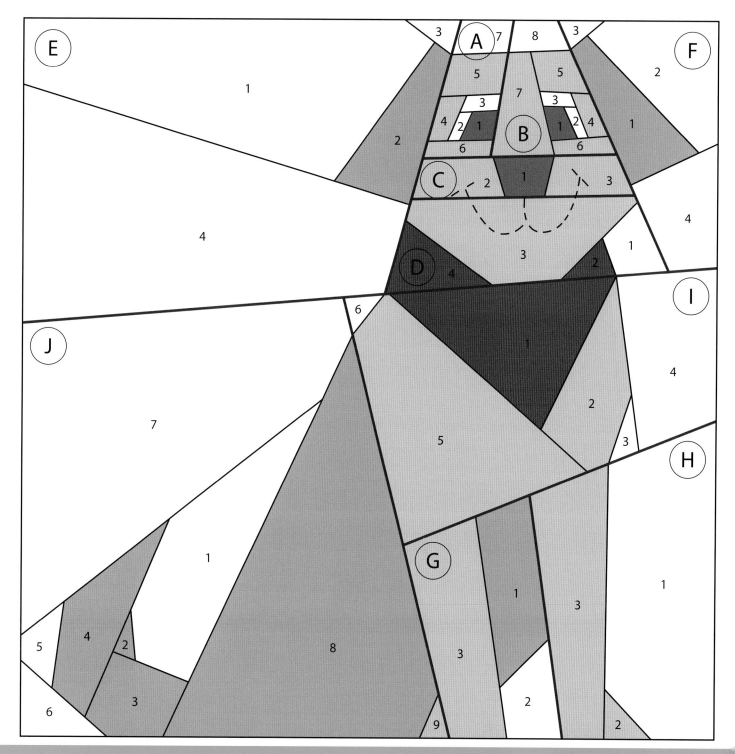

DOG

Materials

- **Scraps:** White, at least 9″ × 11″; dark tan; light tan; red; black; white
- **Embroidery floss:** Black

Directions

For detailed directions, refer to Paper-Piecing Basics (page 7).

1. Make 4 copies of the pattern (A/D/J, B/E/H, C/I, F/G).

2. Cut around each segment, adding ¼″ seam allowances.

3. Paper piece each segment.

4. Connect the segments: A to B; A/B to C to D; A/B/C/D to E to F; G to H; G/H to I; G/H/I to J; A–F to G–J.

5. Trim the block to 8″ × 8″.

6. Hand stitch the mouth with black embroidery floss.

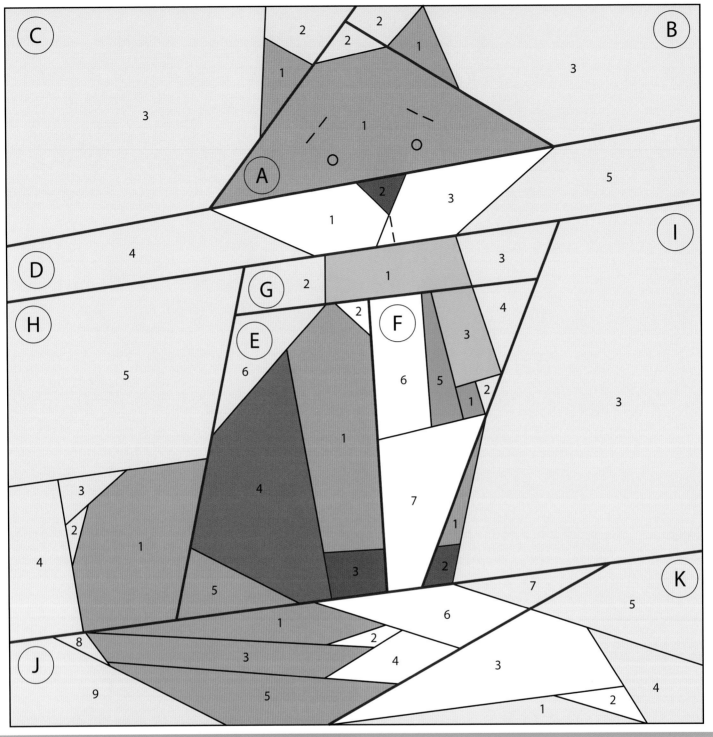

FOX

Materials

- **Scraps:** Turquoise, at least 9″ × 11″; black; orange-brown; red-brown; white; green; dark green
- **Embroidery floss:** Black

Directions

For detailed directions, refer to Paper-Piecing Basics (page 7).

1. Make 5 copies of the pattern (A/G/J, B/H/F/K, C/E, D, I).

2. Cut around each segment, adding ¼″ seam allowances.

3. Paper piece each segment.

4. Connect the segments: A to B; A/B to C; A/B/C to D; E to F; E/F to G to H to I; J to K; A–D to E–I to J/K.

5. Trim the block to 8″ × 8″.

6. Using black embroidery floss, hand stitch the mouth and eyebrows and embroider French knots for the eyes.

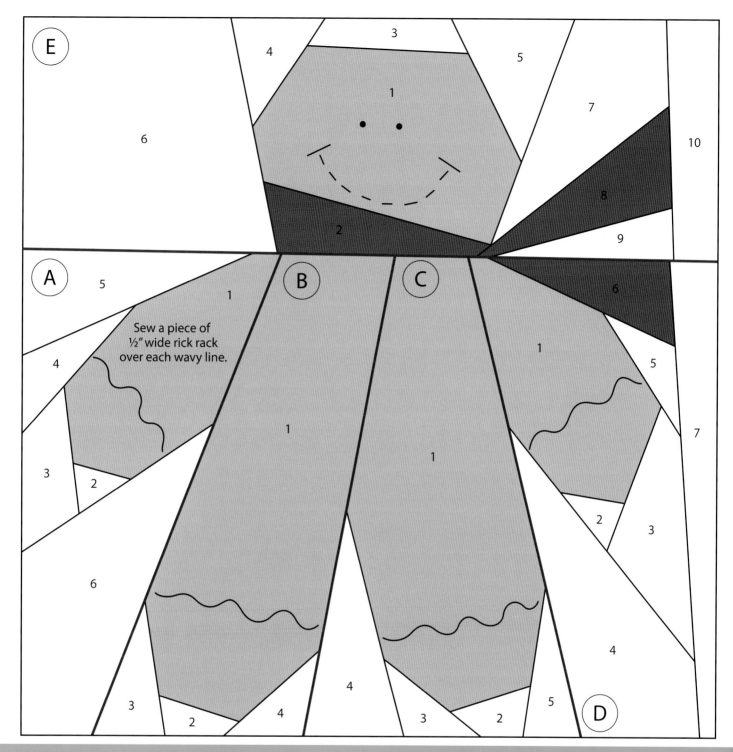

Sew a piece of ½" wide rick rack over each wavy line.

GINGERBREAD

Materials

- **Scraps:** White, at least 9″ × 11″; red; brown
- **Rickrack:** White, ½″ wide
- **Embroidery floss:** Black

Directions

For detailed directions, refer to Paper-Piecing Basics (page 7).

1. Make 3 copies of the pattern (A/C, B/D, E).

2. Cut around each segment, adding ¼″ seam allowances.

3. Pin the #1 fabric in place. Position and pin a piece of ½″ white rickrack over the wavy line, as shown in the #1 piece in Segments A, B, C, D. Hold the pattern up to a window or light source to find the correct position. Stitch rickrack in place. Paper piece each segment.

4. Connect the segments: A to B to C to D; A–D to E.

5. Trim the block to 8″ × 8″.

6. Using black embroidery floss, hand stitch the mouth and embroider French knots for the eyes.

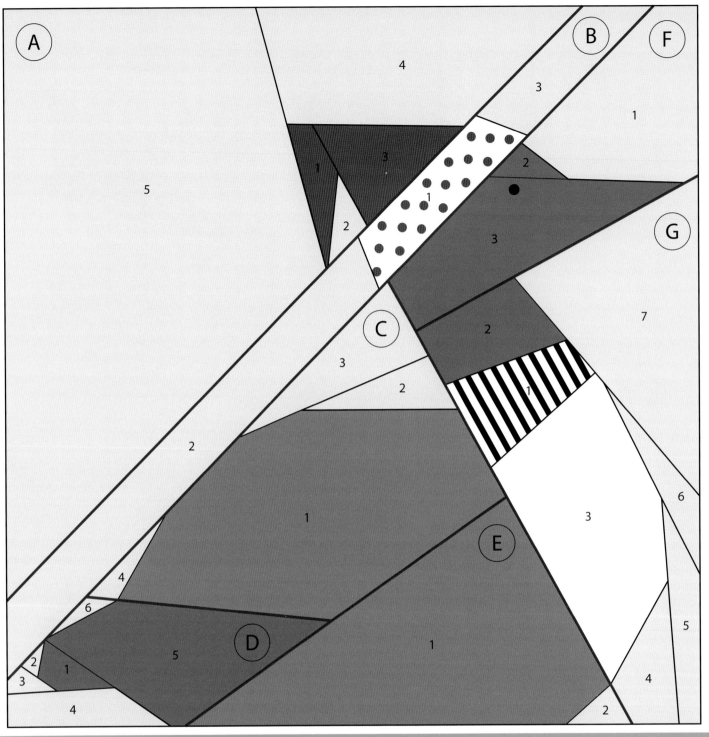

LOON

Materials

- **Scraps:** Turquoise, at least 9″ × 11″; black; white; black polka dot; black stripe; red; red stripe
- **Embroidery floss:** White

Directions

For detailed directions, refer to Paper-Piecing Basics (page 7).

1. Make 4 copies of the pattern (A/C, B, E/F, D/G).

2. Cut around each segment, adding ¼″ seam allowances.

3. Paper piece each segment.

4. Connect the segments: A to B; C to D; C/D to E; F to G; C–E to F/G; A/B to C–G.

5. Trim the block to 8″ × 8″.

6. Hand stitch a French knot for the eye with white embroidery floss.

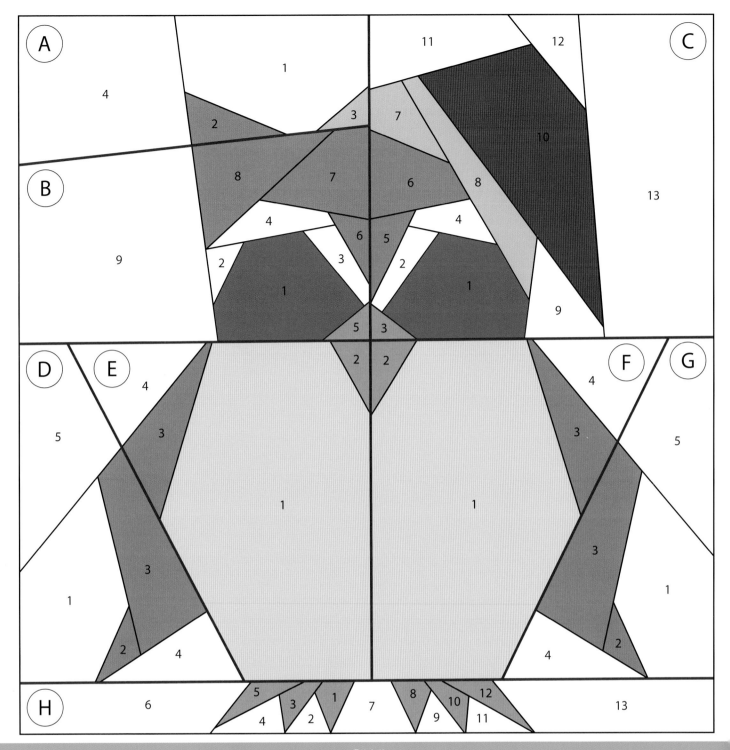

OWL

Materials

- **Scraps:** White, at least 9″ × 11″; black; light brown; brown; green; red; orange

Directions

For detailed directions, refer to Paper-Piecing Basics (page 7).

1. Make 4 copies of the pattern (A/D/F, B/G, C/H, E).

2. Cut around each segment, adding ¼″ seam allowances.

3. Paper piece each segment.

4. Connect the segments: A to B; A/B to C; D to E to F to G; A/B/C to D–G to H.

5. Trim the block to 8″ × 8″.

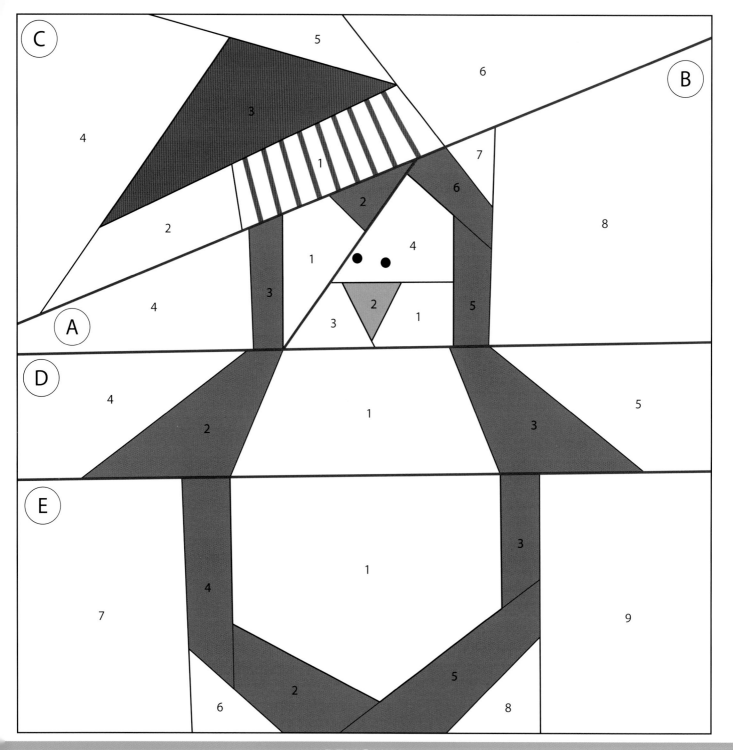

PENGUIN

Materials

- **Scraps:** White, at least 9″ × 11″; white-on-white print; red; black; orange; red stripe
- **Embroidery floss:** Black

Directions

For detailed directions, refer to Paper-Piecing Basics (page 7).

1. Make 3 copies of the pattern (A/E, C/D, B).

2. Cut around each segment, adding ¼″ seam allowances.

3. Paper piece each segment.

4. Connect the segments: A to B to C; A/B/C to D to E.

5. Trim the block to 8″ × 8″.

6. Hand stitch French knots for the eyes with black embroidery floss.

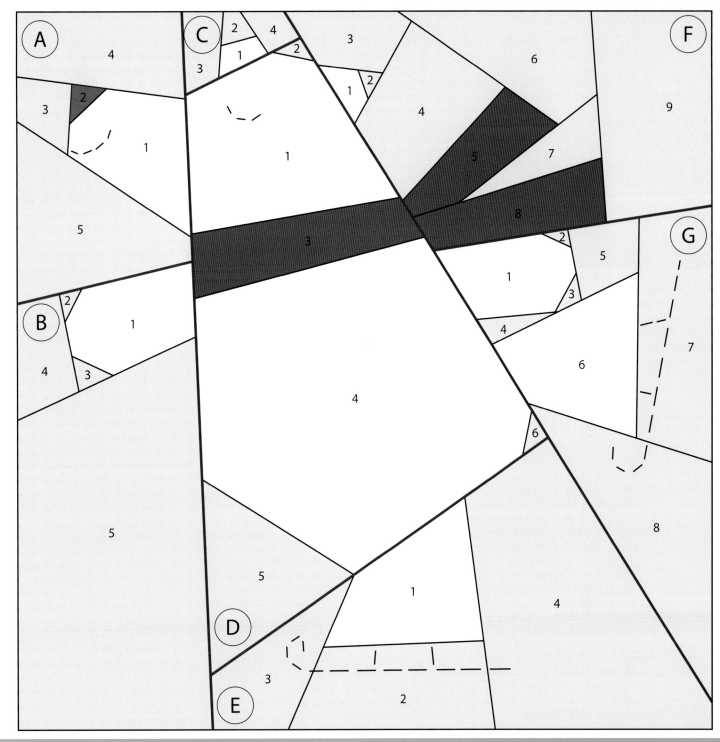

POLAR BEAR SKATING

Materials

- **Scraps:** Turquoise, at least 9″ × 11″; white; black; red
- **Embroidery floss:** Black

Directions

For detailed directions, refer to Paper-Piecing Basics (page 7).

1. Make 3 copies of the pattern (A/E/F, B/C/G, D).

2. Cut around each segment, adding ¼″ seam allowances.

3. Paper piece each segment.

4. Connect the segments: A to B; C to D to E; F to G; A/B to C/D/E to F/G.

5. Trim the block to 8″ × 8″.

6. Hand stitch the mouth, eye, and skates with black embroidery floss.

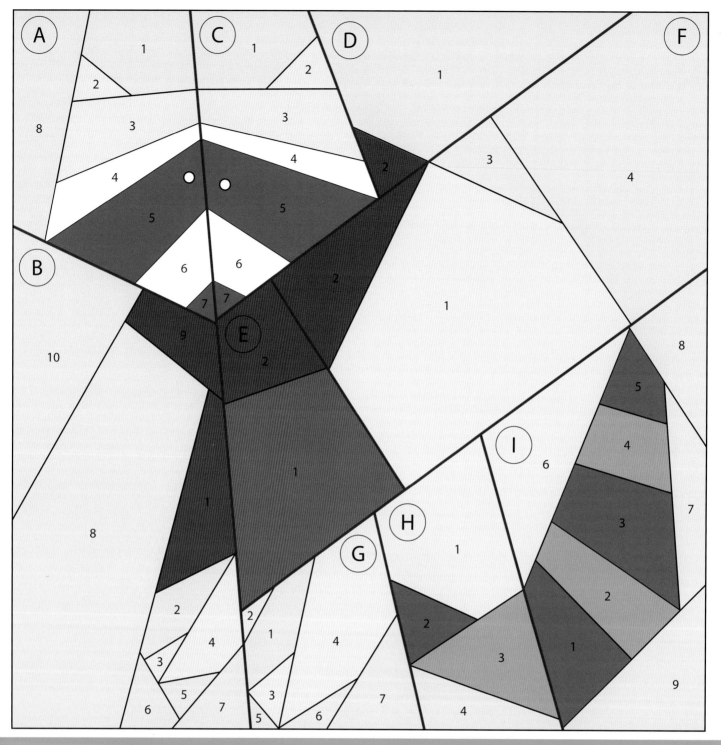

RACCOON

Materials

- **Scraps:** Turquoise, at least 9″ × 11″; black; white; gray; dark gray; red; dark red
- **Embroidery floss:** White

Directions

For detailed directions, refer to Paper-Piecing Basics (page 7).

1. Make 4 copies of the pattern (A/D/G/I, B/F, C/H, E).

2. Cut around each segment, adding ¼″ seam allowances.

3. Paper piece each segment.

4. Connect the segments: A to B; C to D; E to F; G to H to I; C/D to E/F to G/H/I; A/B to C–I.

5. Trim the block to 8″ × 8″.

6. Hand stitch French knots for the eyes with white embroidery floss.

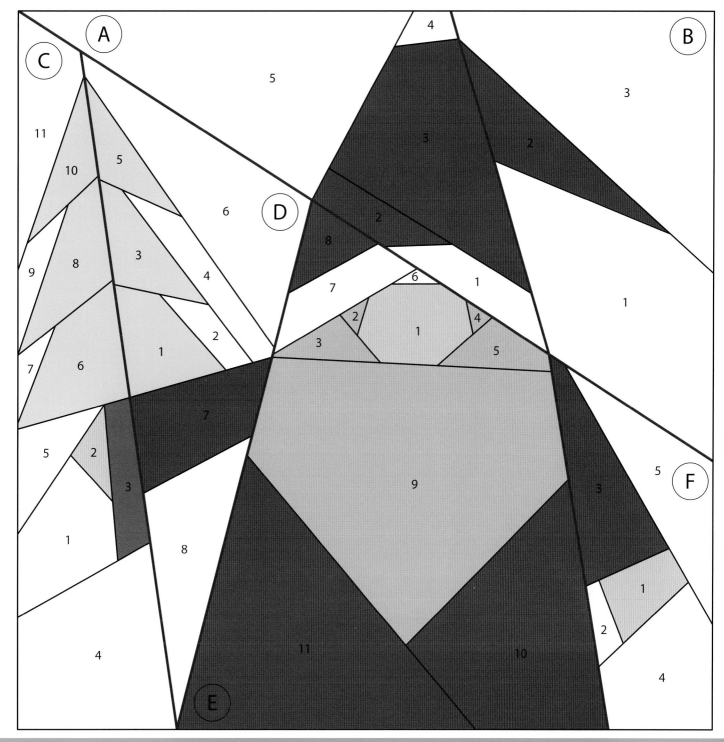

SANTA WITH TREE

Materials

- **Scraps:** White, at least 9″ × 11″; white-on-white print; red; green; brown; peach; gray

Directions

For detailed directions, refer to Paper-Piecing Basics (page 7).

1. Make 4 copies of the pattern (A, B/D, C/F, E).

2. Cut around each segment, adding ¼″ seam allowances.

3. Paper piece each segment.

4. Connect the segments: A to B; C to D to E to F; A/B to C/D/E/F.

5. Trim the block to 8″ × 8″.

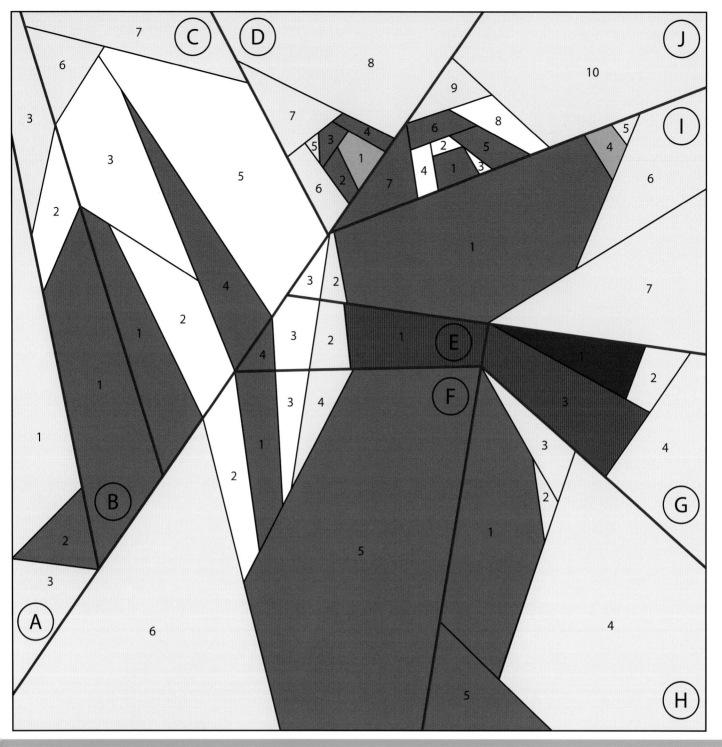

SKUNK

Materials

• **Scraps:** Turquoise, at least 9″ × 11″; white; black; dark gray; red; dark red; pink

Directions

For detailed directions, refer to Paper-Piecing Basics (page 7).

1. Make 4 copies of the pattern (A/C/G, B/D/E, F/I, H/J).

2. Cut around each segment, adding ¼″ seam allowances.

3. Paper piece each segment.

4. Connect the segments: A to B to C to D; E to F; G to H; E/F to G/H; E/F/G/H to I to J; A/B/C/D to E–J.

5. Trim the block to 8″ × 8″.

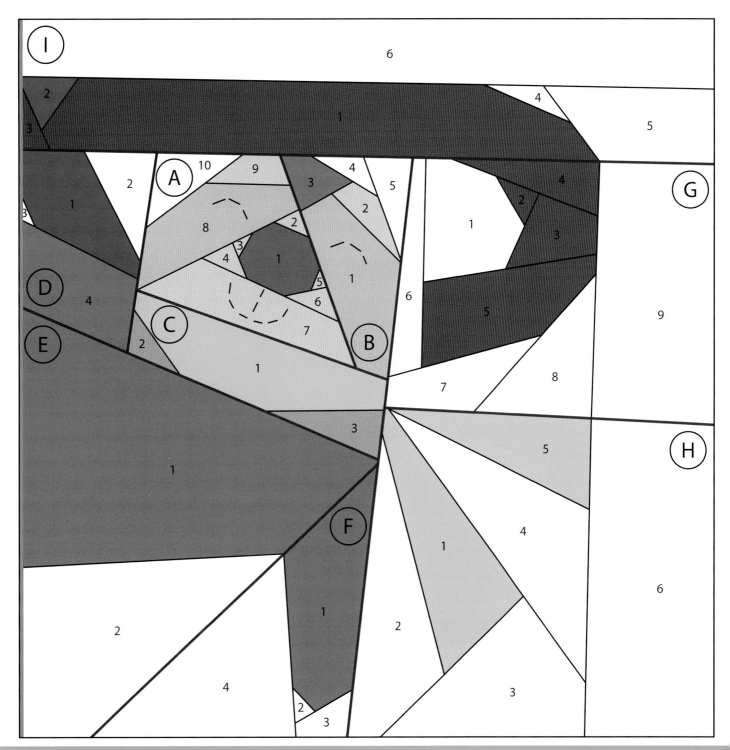

SLOTH WITH CANDY CANE, PART 1

Materials

- **Scraps:** White, at least 9″ × 11″; brown; dark brown; gray; peach; black; green; red
- **Embroidery floss:** Black

Directions

For detailed directions, refer to Paper-Piecing Basics (page 7).

1. Make 4 copies of the pattern (A/F/G, C/I, B/D/H, E).

2. Cut around each segment, adding ¼″ seam allowances.

3. Paper piece each segment.

4. Connect the segments: A to B to C to D to E to F; G to H; A–F to G/H, A–H to I.

5. Trim ¼″ from the blue line.

6. Hand stitch the eyes and mouth with black embroidery floss.

7. Continue to Sloth with Candy Cane, Part 2 (next page).

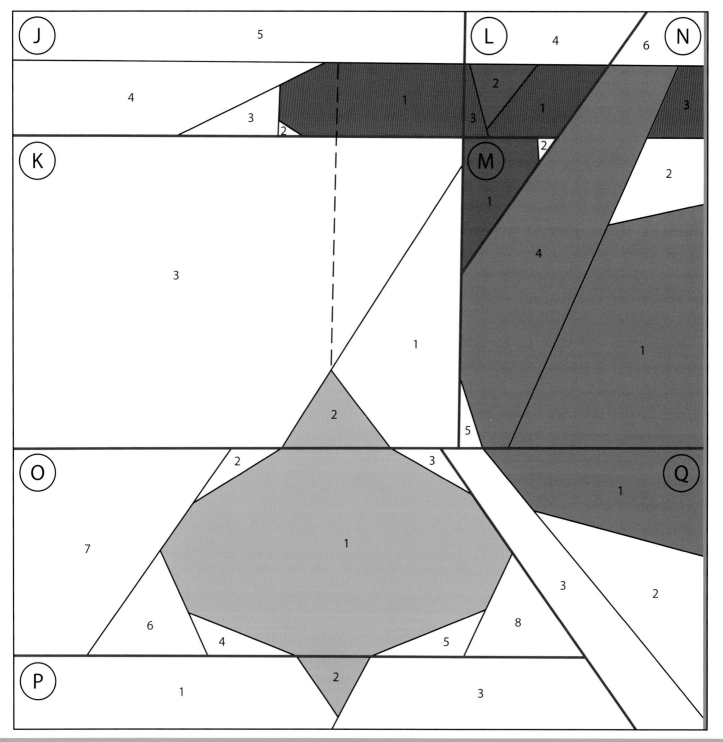

SLOTH WITH CANDY CANE, PART 2

Materials

- **Scraps:** White, at least 9″ × 11″; dark brown; light brown; red; turquoise
- **Embroidery floss:** Black

Directions

For detailed directions, refer to Paper-Piecing Basics (page 7).

1. Make 4 copies of the pattern (J/N/P, K, L/Q, M/O).

2. Cut around each segment, adding ¼″ seam allowances.

3. Paper piece each segment.

4. Connect the segments: J to K; L to M to N; J/K to L/M/N; O to P to Q; J–N to O/P/Q.

5. Trim ¼″ from the blue line. Match and sew Part 1 to Part 2 on the blue lines.

6. Trim the block to 8″ × 15½″.

7. Hand stitch the ornament string with black embroidery floss.

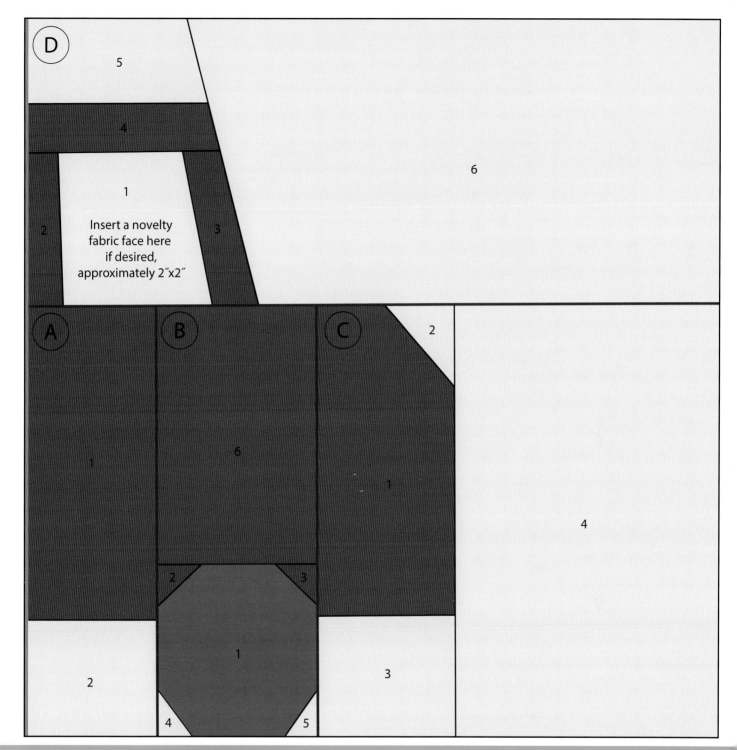

SNOWMAN IN TRUCK, PART 1

Materials

- **Scraps:** Turquoise, at least 9″ × 11″; red; black
- **Novelty fabric:** 2″ × 2″ piece for window, if desired

Directions

For detailed directions, refer to Paper-Piecing Basics (page 7).

1. Make 3 copies of the pattern (A/C, B, D).
2. Cut around each segment, adding ¼″ seam allowances.
3. Paper piece each segment.
4. Connect the segments: A to B to C; A/B/C to D.
5. Trim ¼″ from the blue line.
6. Continue to Snowman in Truck, Part 2 (next page).

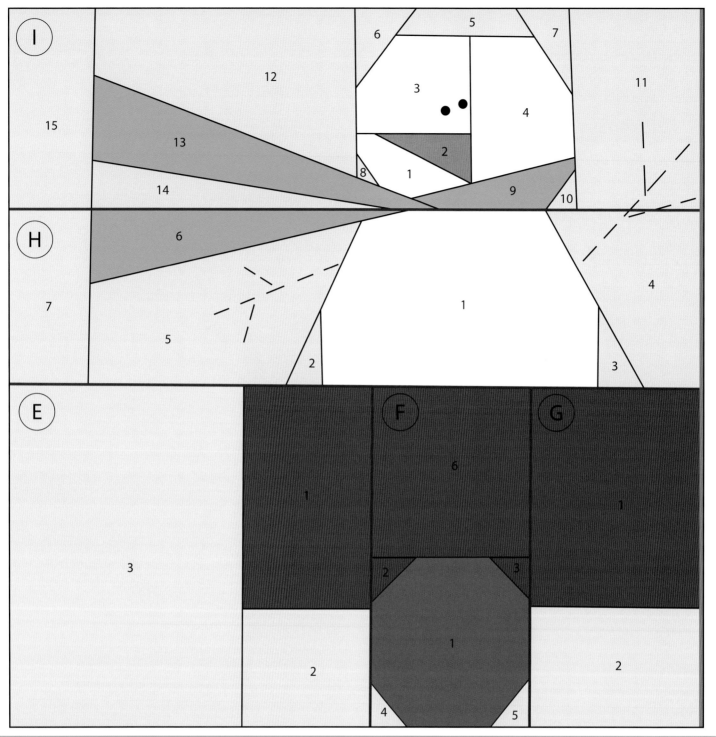

SNOWMAN IN TRUCK, PART 2

Materials
- **Scraps:** Turquoise, at least 9″ × 11″; white; red; black; orange; green
- **Embroidery floss:** Black

Directions

For detailed directions, refer to Paper-Piecing Basics (page 7).

1. Make 3 copies of the pattern (E/G/I, F, H).

2. Cut around each segment, adding ¼″ seam allowances.

3. Paper piece each segment.

4. Connect the segments: E to F to G; E/F/G to H to I.

5. Trim ¼″ from the blue line. Match and sew Part 1 to Part 2 on the blue lines.

6. Trim the block to 8″ × 15½″.

7. Using black embroidery floss, hand stitch the stick arms and embroider French knots for the eyes.

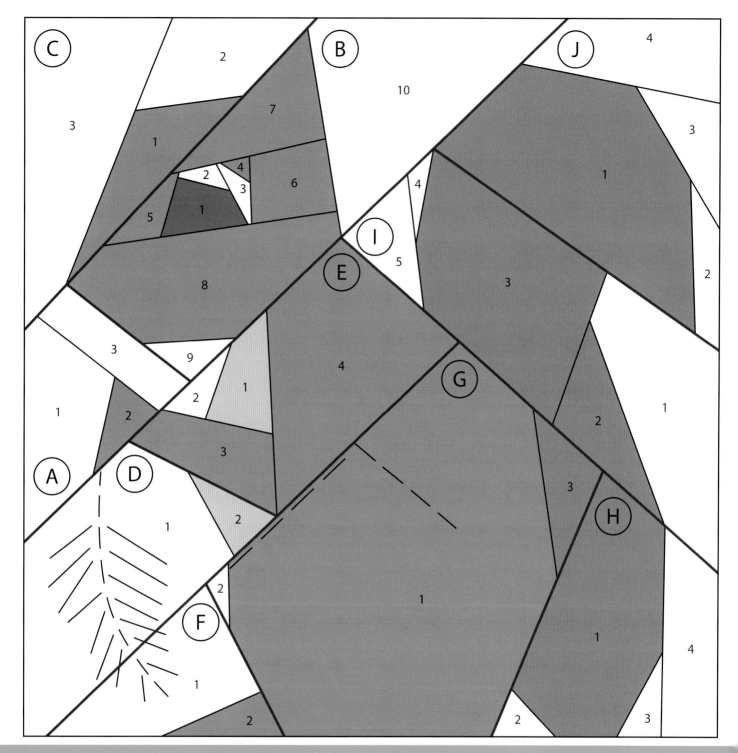

SQUIRREL

Materials

- **Scraps:** White, at least 9″ × 11″; tan; red-brown; dark brown; black
- **Embroidery floss:** Black, green

Directions

For detailed directions, refer to Paper-Piecing Basics (page 7).

1. Make 4 copies of the pattern (A/F/I, B/D/H, C/E/J, G).

2. Cut around each segment, adding ¼″ seam allowances.

3. Paper piece each segment.

4. Connect the segments: A to B; A/B to C; D to E; F to G; D/E to F/G to H; I to J; D−H to I/J; A/B/C to D−J.

5. Trim the block to 8″ × 8″.

6. Hand stitch the stem with black embroidery floss and the needles with green embroidery floss.

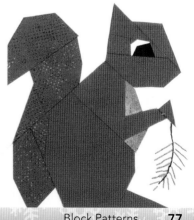

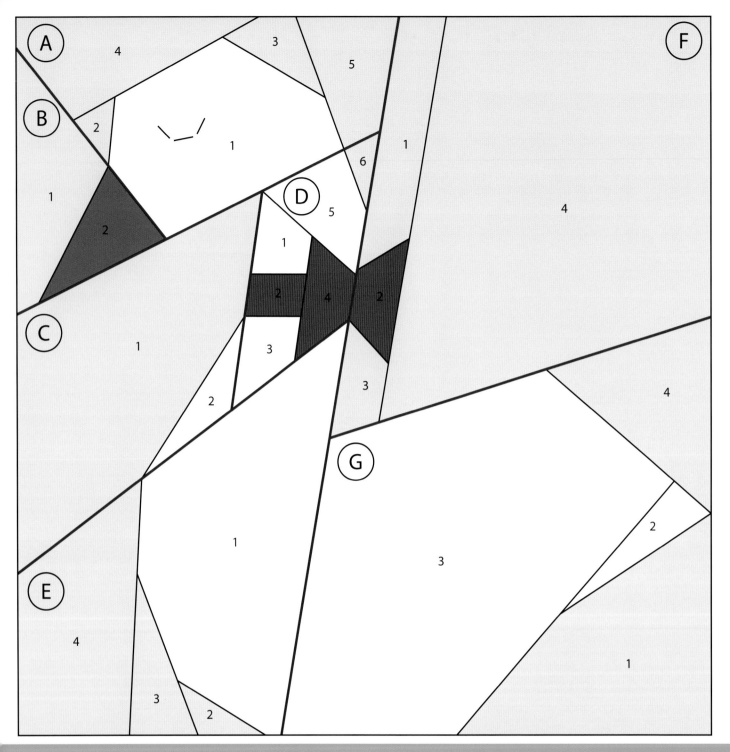

SWAN

Materials

- **Scraps:** Turquoise, at least 9″ × 11″; white; red; dark red; black
- **Embroidery floss:** Black

Directions

For detailed directions, refer to Paper-Piecing Basics (page 7).

1. Make 3 copies of the pattern (A/E, B/D/G, C/F).

2. Cut around each segment, adding ¼″ seam allowances.

3. Paper piece each segment.

4. Connect the segments: A to B; C to D; A/B to C/D; A−D to E; F to G; A−E to F/G.

5. Trim the block to 8″ × 8″.

6. Hand stitch the eye with black embroidery floss.

About the Author

Mary (also known as Marney) Hertel grew up on a small dairy farm in the heart of Wisconsin. Sewing is in her blood, and she likes to say that she has "sewn since birth," starting on her mother's sewing machine at a very early age. After securing her art education job straight out of college, she used her first paycheck to purchase a sewing machine. Soon after, she started to quilt and has never stopped.

Mary's favorite method of quilting became paper piecing after she was introduced to this practice in 2013. The puzzlelike quality of paper piecing appealed to Mary and has quickly become her favorite approach to adding an image to a quilt.

Her quirky animal designs are a nod to 35 years of teaching children's art. "I try to keep my animal designs childlike, but expressive," Mary says. She also strives to offer her readers very easy paper-pieced patterns.

Currently, Mary has seven previously published books, scores of magazine articles, and more than 500 patterns that can be found on Etsy.com and in many quilting stores throughout the United States.

Enjoy her whimsical designs and her easy-to-paper-piece patterns.

Photo by Gail Cameron

Also by Mary Hertel:

Visit Mary online and follow on social media!

Website: madebymarney.com

Facebook: /madebymarney

Pinterest: /maryhertel

Instagram: @madebymarney

Twitter: madebymarney

Etsy: www.etsy.com/shop/ madebymarney

CREATIVE SPARK
ONLINE LEARNING

Quilting courses to become an expert quilter...

From their studio to yours, Creative Spark instructors are teaching you how to create and become a master of your craft. So not only do you get a look inside their creative space, you also get to be a part of engaging courses that would typically be a one or multi-day workshop from the comfort of your home.

Creative Spark is not your one-size-fits-all online learning experience. We welcome you to be who you are, share, create, and belong.

Scan for a gift from us!

creativespark.ctpub.com